Dealing with the Root of Rejection

Finding Your True Identity in Christ

By Angie Stolba

Dealing with the Root of Rejection
Finding Your True Identity in Christ
by Angie Stolba

Printed in the United States of America

ISBN 9781624191435

www.xulonpress.com

Dedication

This book is dedicated to my loving, faithful husband Jeff
who has stood by my side through better and worst.
You have loved me unconditionally, been my
protector and defender, and have seen the
best in me from the very beginning.
You are my best friend, my partner, my mighty oak.
God truly gave me the best when He brought you
into my life to be my husband. Words cannot
express how grateful I am for all the love
and support you've shown me.
I love you!

Acknowledgments

First and foremost, I acknowledge and thank God, my Heavenly Father. He sees the diamond in the rough in each and every one of His children. This book would not be possible without Him. Thank you, Abba, for giving me the strength, courage, and will to write this book—even in the midst of much adversity. To You, Father, and You alone, be all the glory!

To Jeff, my wonderful husband who is truly a "seer" and visionary. When I first shared my life story with you—all the events that took place during my childhood and adolescent years—tears of love and compassion filled your eyes and you said to me, "God is going to use your story to help many women. He's going to use those awful events for His glory."

At that time, your words filled me with such fear, but were so accurate. I remember politely nodding at you as I thought to myself, *No way; no how, will I ever share this story with anyone but you! It's too painful and too shameful.* Wow! Never say "never," huh?! Look what the Lord has done!

To my precious girls who, along with your dad, are my greatest treasures on this earth. I am so proud of each of you and love you all so very much.

Courtney, my firstborn gift, you truly have been blessed with wisdom beyond your years. You partnered with mom through the writing of this book and were a tremendous help. You were strong where I was weak. You lovingly gave countless hours of your time, transcribing my handwritten notebooks into the computer—typing, spell-checking, and helping me through the publishing process. You took on the responsibility of extra housework and cooking meals so mom could press into the Lord and finish this book. How thankful I am for you and to you, and how very proud I am of you. I love you!

Kassidy, my beautiful middle child; what a treasure you are. You are a "helper to all," just as your name states. You have also supported mom throughout the writing of this book. You helped with extra chores and offered your support and encouragement to me through the hard times. You were quick to forgive and brought such joy to my heart. I enjoy our times of walking together, and I'm thrilled to watch you blossom into a wonderful young lady. Watching you dance for the Lord is one of life's greatest gifts to me. You are so precious to me. I love you!

Karissa, my sweet girl; how can it be that you're growing up so fast? You fill my heart with so much joy! Your bubbling laugh and sparkling blue eyes are such a delight to me. I love hearing you sing sweet, pure songs to the Lord. Always keep singing. You have been such a trooper throughout this entire book process, even when you didn't always understand when mommy was "writing." You were quick to adapt and understand when I couldn't always answer your questions or play with you during my writing time. Your love and compassion for animals blesses me. You took on the responsibility of caring for our dogs while I wrote—entertaining them and taking them outside. Thank you for all your help! You are such a special part of our family. I love you!

To Jen Miller, aka Sara, author of *Now I Lay Me Down to Sleep: The Story of Sara.* My sincere thank you and honor for standing by my side from the first written pages of this book. You recognized the potential in my story, even when it was very unrefined. You mentored me in my writing skills while continuing to be a wonderful friend and inspiration to me. You truly have a heart to see me and all women become all God intended us to be. Thank you for the countless hours of editing, and walking with me through the entire book-writing process. This book would not be what it is today without God's work through you. Thank you, my friend, for using your talents and skills for His glory. May He richly bless you for all that you've sown into me. Much love and thanks.

To my Bible study girls: Stephanie, Missy, Angela, and Jennifer. Thank you each for all the love, support, and encouragement you've given me. Thank you for all your prayers for me and the priceless gift of your friendship. I love each one of you.

To Jenny Morse, my "bestie." Our friendship has certainly survived the test of time. You are such a gift to me and I'm so thankful and blessed how God has continued to grow and strengthen our friendship through the years. Even living miles apart, I can pick up the phone at any given time and connect with you as easily as ever. I love sharing our life journeys together. Thank you for all your love, support, and friendship. You are a true gem and I thank God for you!

To June Moore, aka Mama June. Thank you for all the time you put into the early transcription of this book and the hours of final proofreading. I deeply appreciate your words of encouragement to me along the way about this book. Thank you for being a part of this process. You're a special lady and friend. May God richly bless you!

A special thank you to photographer Heather Lockwood for taking my photo for this book, and for our wonderful family photos as well. Thanks for using your gifts and talents to bless others and bring glory to the Lord! May God continue to prosper you in everything you do.

Forward

Once in a while, a book comes along that you know is inspired by the mind of God to help many people. *Dealing with the Root of Rejection* is such a book.

Angie has written this life testimony from her heart. Through this book she reveals how she dealt with and became free from brokenness that many seek to stuff down and keep hidden. Not only does she come clean on intimate details of her life, but also gives important facts why many of life's worst decisions happen. *Dealing with the Root of Rejection* also goes deeper to show us the road to forgiveness and recovery.

Read and learn from this book. Learn how to handle your own brokenness and how to help others with theirs.

We're all broken in various areas of our lives. Sin does this. Having the courage to own our brokenness and sin, and beg forgiveness of God and others, leads to freedom in our daily lives.

Special thanks should be given to the support of her wonderful husband Jeff, for encouraging and helping Angie to come to grips with the story of her life and put it into print. Having known both Angie and Jeff for many of the years of this story, it's an honor to be asked to write this forward.

Thank you, Angie, for your courage in writing. May God bless you and bring personal freedom to all who read this book.

John King
Senior Pastor
Riverside Community Church, Peoria IL

Table of Contents

Introduction

D*ealing with the Root of Rejection* is a very personal look inside of my life journey.

While writing this book was one of the hardest things I've ever done, it has also been one of the most fulfilling, knowing that rejection and fear of man no longer has a grip on me.

In my personal experience, being free from rejection was certainly not something I experienced sudden victory over, but it is something I've had to walk out on a daily basis. The Lord, in His loving kindness, has been by my side through this entire process, relentlessly pursuing me to not just cover up and deal only with the symptoms of rejection, but to be strong and courageous to truly deal with the *root.*

We cannot truly have victory and find our true identity until we've dealt with and conquered the root of rejection.

It is my hope and prayer, by me sharing my story, that you'll be encouraged that God *can* set the captives free and transform thoughts and behavior patterns which have been deeply embedded for years. All He requires is our trust and obedience.

His love and faithfulness is *everlasting.*

Angie Stolba
Author

Chapter 1

The Root of Rejection . . . My Story

One of my earliest childhood memories was being at children's church, and being called "goofy."

Words pierce. They define us as good or bad, valued or unworthy. Words are seeds which go down to the deepest core of a person's heart. The seeds of rejection were planted in my heart from a very early age. I believed in my heart and mind that I truly was goofy and different, and I'd think, *What's wrong with me? Why don't I fit in with the other kids?*

A prominent boy at church tagged me "goofy." The name stuck. Before long, other children were chiming in as well. I hated being called that. Finally, I gathered up enough courage to timidly approach the teacher, struggling to put into words just how terrible the name-calling made me feel. It's hard for a child to articulate those feelings. But under the teacher's direction, the boy who had started the verbal abuse apologized to me. He told me that they had just been "joking around" and I shouldn't get my feelings hurt over that.

That's when shame linked arms with rejection inside me. Yes, they had been joking around, but at *my* expense. I tried to shrug it all off, but the seeds of rejection had been planted in me.

Other than telling the teacher, I never told anyone else about being called goofy and how awful it made me feel. I felt like I had no one in whom I could confide. I didn't share with my mom or dad because, although they were loving parents and I knew they loved me, our family didn't openly talk much about our feelings. Talking about intimate things was not encouraged, and there weren't many displays of physical affection. So, for the most part, I kept my feelings inside. Later in life, I would see how hiding my feelings had adversely affected me through many years.

I would also learn that Satan is a liar and uses abuse of every kind to destroy our hearts and put us on a collision course. The Bible says he is ". . . the father of lies" (John 8:44). I believed, even at a young age, that he was trying to abort my true destiny by watering those seeds of rejection which were continually planted in me by my peers and others.

I felt so sad and discouraged at church—a place where everyone was supposed to feel accepted and loved.

My dad was a good dad. He was an excellent provider, but his job took him away from home a lot while I was growing up. Whenever he was home, though, our family ate dinner together and attended church together. Due to his hard work to provide for our family, I didn't experience the closeness or intimacy with him that I longed for. This also fed my growing feelings of rejection, from seeds into a "root."

School was difficult, too. In elementary school, making good grades was a struggle for me. I had to work really hard to just get Cs. Most of my classes were mainstream, but I had math and science in Special Ed.

Kids can be so cruel.

I was labeled as a slow learner and made fun of for being "one of those kids."

The rejection and shame grew stronger and stronger inside me. All the while, my heart was bleeding—longing and hoping for someone to affirm me and find value in me. It seemed the harder I tried to gain others' approval, the more they disapproved of me.

I especially dreaded gym class. One day, two students were taking turns choosing teammates. In the end, there were three kids left to choose from. As usual, without fail, I was the last one chosen. Oh, the humiliation I felt!

Rejection, shame, and humiliation were the three strands woven together inside me as a growing and deepening root. Although referring to people banning together for strength, the same principle of Ecclesiastes 4:12 (NIV) applies to whatever is planted inside us, good or bad: "A cord of three strands is not quickly broken." How very true.

The grade school years were not at all fun for me, to say the least. The ugly, three-stranded root of rejection was growing stronger and deeper in me, distorting, confusing, and destroying who God had originally created me to be from before the day I was born.

Growing into adolescence I was physically a "late-bloomer:" overly thin, gangly, and prone to acne breakouts. The kids laughed at me and called me "zit face," further feeding the root of rejection inside me.

In middle school, I longed to fit in and finally be accepted by my peers; so I began to experiment with my hair and makeup. It seemed as though, on the outside, the ugly duckling was finally disappearing and a beautiful swan was emerging.

I was determined I would be liked and accepted by the other kids. So, on the first day of eighth grade, I went to school with my new look: hair curled and styled, makeup neatly in place . . . Gone were the "plain Jane" clothes, replaced with fitted, fashionable name brands. I saw heads turn in my direction in the halls and heard the whispers, "Did you see her? She looks so different!" But on the inside, it was still the same me: insecure, self-conscious, longing, and silently crying out for love and acceptance.

I wanted to forget all the pain and humiliation of my grade school years; so when boys started paying attention to me, the pretty, popular girls let me into their elite circle. I was ready and eager for this newfound attention. *Now I will surely fit in*, I silently assured myself with excitement and anticipation.

I started to mimic them—"the cool kids" I hung out with. I dressed like them and acted like them. I was so desperate and starved for any kind of acceptance and affirmation, by any means opened to me, I consequently began to rebel against my Christian upbringing.

It seemed that the father of lies was gaining the upper hand in my life. I would lie, sneak out with my new friends, and use bad language which I knew was not right. But I wanted to be considered "cool" by my peers. I was doing all I knew to do to numb the ever-growing sadness and hurt gnawing inside me.

I spent a lot of time with one girl in particular. She was pretty, a rebel, and seemed to have it all. I couldn't believe she would even want to be friends with someone like me. Gone were the days of being ridiculed and labeled "goofy" and "dumb." I had found *real* friends—people who would be there for me. I was beginning to feel a little better, but I was still highly insecure.

I became extremely loyal to my new friends. I would drop everything when they called. I was changing the *real me* to be accepted by that group, and I was letting go of the Godly values taught to me and mirrored by my parents and our church.

One summer day, all dolled up, I walked to the house of a boy who was part of our group. We were really just acquaintances at the time, although we hung out together in group settings. Ben invited me inside and upstairs to his bedroom. "We can just hang out," he told me.

My young, naïve, and ravenous heart leapt. I was excited and in awe that he was flirting with *me* and truly seemed to want to be with me. I had not experienced this before. It was powerful and heady in my hunger for love and acceptance.

"Do you want a wine cooler?" he asked.

Not wanting to appear a "Miss Goody Two-shoes," I said yes, although I had seldom had alcohol and was only 15 years old. I felt excited and a little like the rebel I admired. While we were sitting in his room, drinking wine coolers with rock-and-roll playing in the background, his intentions became clear.

Looking back, as an adult, I see that what happened next would forever alter the course of my life.

God has given us the gift of free will and has
set "choices" before us.
He pleads with and beckons us to choose His freedom in our lives
by making Godly choices which will honor Him and protect
us; however, the choices are ultimately our own.

One thing led to another and by my own free will I gave myself to Ben—completely. I gave him my most cherished treasures: my virginity, my purity, my naivety, my trust, my love . . . , my heart. I convinced myself that what we shared was meaningful and believed from that moment on he would always love me, want to be with me, and protect me.

On that life-altering afternoon, I left his house with mixed emotions. Part of me was very excited, as though I had gained a new freedom and control of my life. No longer was I controlled by those who had hurt me in the past—though I would find out later how the complete opposite was true. But deep in my heart of hearts, I also felt used, scared, unsure . . . , and regretful that I had just given away the most precious parts of me, which I could never, ever get back.

Ben called me during the next couple of weeks. We would talk and flirt with each other but never really spent any quality time together after that life-changing summer afternoon.

One afternoon, a friend from our group knocked on my front door. "Hey!" she exclaimed, all cheerful, with a light attitude. "Jill wants to meet you at the park. Just to talk with you," she added as a quick explanation.

Immediately I felt uneasy; but I shook it off, believing these kids were my friends. *What could be the harm in walking down to the park? I brushed at my discomfort. I'm sure everything will be fine*, I attempted to assure myself. I had decided to go, against my feelings that something might be wrong in this situation.

I lived only a few houses up from the park, so it took no time at all to get there. Immediately upon arriving, I had an overwhelming sense of dread. Truth was, Jill was known as "the tough girl," a recognized bully, and she was standing in the middle of the playground—waiting for me.

The rest of my friends in our group were perched on various pieces of playground equipment, waiting expectantly, as if to watch some kind of show or event. I was filled with dread and fear. I had taken the bait; another poor choice.

Suddenly Jill pushed and shoved me, making a big production about what was going to take place: beat me up. She started rambling at me, then yelling as she shoved me, accusing me of causing trouble for her friend Ben. She demanded that I should leave him alone, and further harassed me by saying I had no business even being around him.

I was stunned!

I was also confused because Ben was the one who had initially pursued *me*. My mind raced; I couldn't think of anything I had done to make her that upset with me—other than what had taken place between Ben and me two weeks earlier. But to my knowledge, Jill and Ben were just friends. I didn't understand what was happening. Was she *jealous* of me? Or was this just an excuse on her part to start trouble for me and give her a reason to fight me to gain attention for herself? She seemed to thrive on her reputation as a fearless bully.

I saw no way out.

I had become her next victim.

Desperately, I looked over to my friends, silently pleading with them to come to my rescue. Then I saw him—Ben—the one who I was convinced loved me and would surely rescue me from this girl's cruelty. But he wouldn't even look directly at me; he made no eye contact with me. He just sat there and did nothing to come to my defense.

Oh, the devastation and realization of what was happening to me! Not only was I facing a bully, in my humiliation in front of all my 'friends,' but Ben—the one I had put all my hope and trust in and had given *all* of myself to—was not only rejecting all we had shared together but was cruelly rejecting me. More than the physical pain I was experiencing at Jill's brutal hand, deep anguish filled my heart as I realized the boy I loved cared nothing at all for me. That was a harder blow than the one Jill would soon give me.

The others, who just sat there, my closest circle of 'friends,' had betrayed me in the cruelest way imaginable. They were not going to help me, but, in fact, seemed *entertained* at what was taking place as Jill pushed me again then hit me, making a spectacle of me before their very eyes.

It only took a few good hits from her before I found myself lying limp on the concrete walkway. Once down, she grabbed and yanked my hair and slammed my face into the sidewalk—again and again. The beating seemed endless and my mind "disconnected" from the rest of the beating.

It wasn't until I was an adult that I learned about dissociation: our body's God-created ability to block one's mind while in (or after) a very traumatic event. It's often referred to as "shock;" going into shock, being in shock. While Jill had continued to punch me, it was as if the Lord had wrapped me inside His invisible bubble, protecting my mind from the awful violation taking place against me.

When I began to come out of the dissociative state, I saw Jill looking over to her friends. Her words ring clear in my mind to this day: "Well guys, has she had enough?" They just sat there and stared at her, saying nothing. With that, she gave me one final kick in my side and it was over. They all left me lying there; beaten, bruised, bleeding, disoriented, confused, and . . . totally broken in spirit.

My world had come crashing down in a matter of minutes. I was totally rejected, totally heartbroken, totally shamed, humiliated, and violated, *and* physically wounded. I lay there bleeding and aching in every way as they all went on their way.

Totally abandoned.

My head was throbbing with pain from being banged repeatedly against the concrete, and my heart and spirit was shattered. I had a long, bleeding cut along my cheek and my whole body ached with pain and bruising from Jill's shoving, punching, and banging my head into the concrete, and that final kick. But even worse than the horrific physical pain was the emotional agony I was suffering. I felt as if I had just experienced the ultimate betrayal.

How could my friends—especially him*—do this to me?* I had given Ben all of me. He was supposed to love and protect me; but he had done nothing! I felt as though I had experienced a horrible nightmare, and wished it had simply been that.

The nightmare didn't end there.

Bleeding and crying, somehow I was able to pick myself up and stumble the short distance to my house, only to find it empty. My mom and dad were both working and my sister was at a friend's house. I managed to telephone my mom and she immediately came home, along with my sister.

When my mom arrived, she was stunned by what she saw and by what had happened to me. She took me to a prompt care, concerned about a possible concussion and my other injuries.

That night, safely back home with my family, we were unprepared and surprised by a sudden pounding on our front door. By the aggressive hammering, I just knew it was Jill. Once again I was filled with terror. My mom and dad went to the door and opened it, and Jill angrily demanded to see me.

My mom and dad told her to leave our property.

Shouting at my mom, and as though possessed, Jill grabbed her around the neck and began to choke her. My dad immediately pulled her off and pushed her away, into the yard, telling her to leave and that he was going to call the police.

As she ran away, she looked back over her shoulder and shouted, "You've just signed your daughter's death warrant!"

Stunned and enraged, my dad telephoned the police who arrived a short time later.

There were no more direct incidences with Jill; but after that day, my life grew increasingly worse.

Jill's beating and humiliating me at the park sparked all kinds of talk at school, and I became an easy target for other bullies to pick on. I began to get threats and hear rumors in the hallways about others who wanted to beat me up. I lived in constant fear, turmoil, and worry.

As the weeks passed, I dropped into a deeper depression and began to doubt my life's purpose. *What's wrong with me?* I continually asked myself, believing there *must* be something terribly wrong with me for the years of ridicule and rejection that followed me. I felt like such an outcast among my peers.

The long bus ride home from high school each day was agony as the kids' voices mocked and taunted me. One of the names they called me was "Agnes of God." I had no idea what that meant or why they would call me that. The only conclusion I came to was that my family went to church and my dad was bold in his Christian beliefs. He was always sharing the gospel.

The boys on the bus who called me Agnes of God lived behind our house, so it was easy for them to hear the loud volume of Christian teaching and music tapes my dad played regularly. I knew they could hear the tapes every day because I could hear them laughing beyond my bedroom window where I would sit and look outside. Calling me that degrading name was just another cruel way a growing number of kids humiliated me and the root of rejection inside me grew stronger.

On the school bus, I would sit as close to the front as possible, hoping the bus driver would see the bullying and possibly come to my defense. The kids who called me names and harassed me generally sat as far to the back of the bus as they could. I thought I would be safest sitting in the front near the driver. Unfortunately, the bus driver was either unaware of their constant, abusive teasing or simply chose to do nothing about it. I had grown far too insecure, timid, and ashamed to speak to the driver, and feared she would also reject me and not come to my aid.

Just like my children's church experience many years earlier, I felt the same sense of helplessness and shame. I no longer had any courage at all to tell those in authority near me—not even my parents—what was happening to me daily. The root of rejection had completely ensnared me. I felt trapped and helpless.

Riding the bus home from school every day became a growing anxiety which filled me with daily fear and dread.

One afternoon on the bus, the kids in the back were calling me names and poking fun at me, as usual. I hated it, but did my best to tune out their voices (to no avail). Suddenly, without warning, I felt something hit me on the back of the head. To my shock and shame, I discovered it was a chewed-up piece of gum from one of the boys. Tears of anger and humiliation burned my eyes as I slumped further down in my seat and began to uncoil the gum which had become imbedded in my long, dark hair. All the while, I heard their snickering as they continued to poke fun at what had just taken place. Once again I had become their target, and no one came to my defense.

I counted the minutes until the bus dropped me off at my stop. All the while, I hoped I could make it safely to my house without further embarrassment and ridicule. School had become a nightmare for me. The name-calling and bullying had begun to spin out of control since that awful day at the park with Jill.

Unknowingly, I participated in my own further demise as I allowed negative thoughts and feelings about myself to constantly bombard me. There was so much ugliness toward me by others' words and actions, and so much ugliness inside me, that I believed I was truly worthless.

Depression, despair, and a sense of hopelessness had settled over me like an ever-present dark night. There seemed to be no way out of my despair. I had no friends and no one in whom I could confide or trust. Life was cruel and unfair. As quickly as I had gotten into a "cool" clique, I was out of it. My problems had plummeted from bad to abominable—the worst. The root of rejection had grown despairingly deep. It was a festering, ugly monster that was devouring me. I couldn't take the pain of rejection any longer.

I contemplated suicide.

Taking my life; ending it all. No more bullying; no more pain.

I thought about taking a bottle of pills, but when it finally came down to that moment, I was too fearful of death; and I thought about my family: my mom, my dad, my sister, my grandparents . . . those who I knew truly loved me.

Deep down I realized I didn't want to end my life; I just wanted to escape the torment I was living with every day.

I believed it was the hand of God on me that prevented me from taking the pills, just as He had been there with me in the park, preserving my mind during that awful beating, humiliation, and rejection.

So was the case in the valley of decision concerning the pills; He was there, urging me to hold on.

Though I could see no hope or promise of a better life, by God's grace I received His courage to tell my mom about the torment I was going through. At my breaking point, I confessed to her that I had been living as a target for bullies, continually being harassed by a growing number of peers. I shared with her how bad things had become and my ever-present thoughts of suicide.

She was stunned. She had had no clue that my school life had become life-threatening.

I had become very good at hiding the realities of my daily school life from my parents. My mom was sick with grief that her daughter was suffering such torment and she hadn't even known. Her eyes were opened to the fact that my daily environment had to change—immediately.

She shared with my dad all that was happening to me at school and the gravity of the situation: their daughter had become suicidal. They knew they had to make some serious changes in my life.

Out of their selfless love and concern for my well-being, they came to the difficult decision that our family needed to move. This meant that my dad had to change jobs, but God had already made the way.

My dad was able to be transferred, with the same employer, to a division three hours away. God had made a way for a fresh, new start.

My parents acted on the promise of Proverbs 3:5-6: "Trust in the LORD with all your heart and do not lean on your own understanding. In all your ways acknowledge Him, and He will make your path straight."

Even though we moved to a new town and new home, I still carried the same debilitating and suffocating wounds inside me. On the inside, there was no fresh start; I still lived where the "father of lies" had bound me: in darkness and despair.

The Word of God, which is truth and light, tells us in Proverbs 23:7, "As he [she] thinks within himself, so he is."

What I didn't realize at the time was that I was also sabotaging myself by *believing* the lies which evil had mirrored to me time and again, through all the years of being bullied. I had grown to see myself as worthless, having no value; therefore, I was continually drawing negative people and experiences to me.

My thinking at that time, though, was still far from this knowledge. My thinking was from an outward perspective: that a new town, a new school, a fresh start would make all the difference.

I began my junior year in a new high school and was sure that I was free from the demons of my past. As I passed boys in the halls, they would smile and flirt with me; and I was like a sponge, soaking up any attention and affirmation I could get. I was desperate for love and acceptance by my peers. Like a drug, I would take acceptance any way I could get it.

Before long, I was on the same dark, slippery path I had run from when our family had moved. I was still just as emotionally needy and wounded as I had been before the move. So the attention from boys was like water to my thirsty soul. Consequently, over time, I had several relationships with boys who ultimately had only one intention. Like a lamb going to slaughter, I followed along, desperate for the cavernous void of hurt and despair within me to be filled.

I became seriously involved in a relationship which lasted for some time; then I found out that he had been cheating on me! When he learned that I knew about his unfaithfulness, he decided he no longer wanted anything to do with me. What little self-worth I had regained after our move was quickly ebbing away again. The harsh tide of victimization was continually eroding the spirit which God had originally created in me. I was surely on a one-way road to destruction.

We can attempt to bury the wounds of our pasts
and try to convince ourselves they're no longer there,
and that we're really "over it." But until we've
dealt with our wounds
at the root, they will always be there, tormenting us,
negatively influencing
our thoughts, decisions, and actions, which we will pass along—
generation to generation.

After several relationships with guys who were only interested in what they could get from me physically, I finally had enough courage to say "I'm done."

I repented to God for all the years I had rebelled against Him and gone on my way. And He removed my sins ". . . as far as the east is from the west" (Psalm 103:12 NIV). I experienced true forgiveness, a true fresh start with my Heavenly Father. And He gave me a peace I had not known before. It had taken me coming to the very end of myself—as low in spirit, mindset, and behavior as I could go—in order to see that God had been there all along, patiently waiting for me.

I got back into church and rejoiced in the knowledge that God knew the *real* me—with the ugly root still strongly intact—and yet He still loved me. Even though I had forsaken Him and had turned my back on His Word and my Christian upbringing, He was still there. He had never abandoned me nor turned His back on me like others had. He promised in His Word that He would never leave me or forsake me, a promise that is stated not only once but *seven* times! (John 14:18; Hebrews 13:5; Deuteronomy 4:31, 31:6, 31:8; Joshua 1:5; 1 Chronicles 28:20)

His Word also says that Jesus is ". . . a friend who sticks closer than a brother" (Proverbs 18:24). Even through my darkest hour—that terrible beating—He had been there, shielding me from the physical pain I should have felt to the end. He had a purpose for my life. After all the years of heartache and torment, I had finally come into ". . . the peace of God, which surpasses all comprehension . . ." (Philippians 4:7).

God truly gives us a peace which this world and the things of it cannot give.

I made a vow to the Lord that I would leave my promiscuous ways behind and follow Him and His Word.

I began to draw on the Godly roots of my Christian upbringing and faith, which my parents had instilled in me. I remembered the prayer my dad had shared with me when I was old enough to understand. From the time I was young girl, he had prayed that God would bring a Spirit-filled Christian young man into my life to be my future husband. My dad, being a man of strong faith, believed that God had a specific man already chosen for me who would be my perfect mate. I chose to believe this too, and I clung to Jeremiah 29:11:

"'For I know the plans I have for you,'
declares the LORD,
'plans for welfare and not for calamity to give you a future and a hope.'"

It's my personal belief that this scripture is a promise for those who have put their faith in Jesus Christ as Savior and who strive to live for God by faith. I also believe that one of the rewards of this scripture is that He will prosper us in many ways as we allow His plans for our lives to unfold.

As I repented to God for my sins, I told Him I believed His Word, and I held tight to the belief that He had created the right man for me and would bring him into my life in His perfect way and time—even though I had severely missed the mark on several occasions. I made a vow to God that I would not even date another man until I knew He had brought the right one to me: His *best* for me.

I was finally on the right track.

The Lord, in His loving kindness and mercy, would allow His plans for my life to come to pass in beautiful and amazing ways. And with His strength and courage, I would eventually be free from the root of rejection.

He reached down from on high and took hold of me;
he drew me out of deep waters.

He rescued me from my powerful enemy,
from my foes, who were too strong for me.

They confronted me in the day of my disaster,
but the Lord was my support.

He brought me out into a spacious place;
he rescued me because he delighted in me.
Psalm 18:16-19 (NIV)

Chapter 2

My Prince Charming

"Let us not lose heart in doing good,
For in due time we will reap if we
do not grow weary."
Galatians 6:9 (NIV)

Months passed—and thankfully, so had my high school years.

I was still enjoying my restored faith and relationship with God as I entered adulthood, but still longed for my future husband. It was the true desire of my heart to have a Godly man in my life. I wondered if this would ever come to pass. I secretly continued to pour out my heart to the Lord, asking Him to bring my future husband into my life.

One night I was bored, sitting at home with nothing to do. My mom invited me to go with her and a few of her friends to a prayer meeting at our small, full-gospel church. Even though I was faithfully living for the Lord and enjoying my restored relationship with Him, I was a little skeptical about going to the prayer meeting, thinking it would be filled with "Holy Rollers." But I finally agreed, convincing myself that I had nothing better to do.

When we arrived, the women there were very kind and had sweet spirits about them. They graciously welcomed me, even though I was much younger than anyone else there. I felt God's presence as the women prayed over each other. It was a very real and tangible experience with God. Prophetic words were being spoken over some of the ladies and God was moving on their hearts in a powerful way.

I sat quietly among a row of chairs, thinking how happy I was for them, when one of the ladies asked if they could pray for me as well. I sheepishly agreed, feeling self-conscious. One of the women prayed for me specifically and began to prophecy over me, confirming that God had heard my prayers about bringing my future husband into my life! The amazing thing was that I had not shared my prayers with anyone except God. Not even my mom. So I knew it was definitely the Spirit of God speaking to me through the woman. She began by saying, "God has heard your prayers, and good things—very good things—are in your future."

I knew exactly what "good things" she spoke of.

Shortly after that experience, my pastor prayed for me and he too prophesied about my future husband. "God has heard your prayers and He is preparing your future husband's heart as well. Soon your paths will cross." The Lord even revealed to him where my future husband was at the time! He said, "God has shown me that the man you're going to marry is just finishing his last courses at Illinois Central College."

I got the chills!

Not only had God heard my prayers, but He was getting ready to answer them and grant the deepest desire of my heart! My mom rejoiced with me, too, over the sheer joy and excitement of God's intimacy in our lives that He would speak so directly through His people.

A couple of months later, I met my future husband.

During those months prior, my parents felt led to begin visiting a new church, and my sister and I went with them and decided to also attend one of their youth services.

I was in the sanctuary with my sister and her friend.

That's when it happened! *I saw him! My future husband!*

From across the sanctuary our eyes locked for the first time!

Although I didn't know in that moment that he was the one, I felt an amazing connection with him as our eyes held for only a moment. I knew there was something special about him, even though we had not even spoken to each other yet.

It was almost impossible for me to focus on the rest of the service. Thoughts of him continually ran through my mind. Sadly, though, I had to leave the service early for a prior commitment. My heart was torn because I longed to stay and get to know him. I was very intrigued by him. Regretfully, I didn't even get a chance to speak with him that night.

My sister and her friend were able to stay after the service, though, and get acquainted with some of the youth group. One of the kids invited the whole group to her house, and my sister and her friend followed along. *He was there!*—my future husband!

Later, when my sister got home, she told me that he had introduced himself to her and her friend as "Jeff."

Jeff. I now knew his name.

She also shared that he had inquired about *me*! "What happened to the other girl who was with you," he'd asked, "the brunette?" I learned he had asked my sister all kinds of questions about me. It was obvious he was just as interested in me as I was in him.

I wanted to be certain we were talking about the same guy I had locked eyes with at the beginning of the service; so she described him to the best of her knowledge, confirming for me that he was, in fact, the same guy. My heart leapt! I could hardly wait to see him again!

The next youth service was scheduled for the following Wednesday; and I made sure I was going to be there, for the *whole* service this time. I was hoping I would see Jeff and we'd get a chance to talk.

When I arrived and went upstairs to the youth room, there he was! He timidly approached me and said, "Hello, would you like a piece of gum?"

At first I wondered if I *needed* a piece of gum! My insecurities were always close at hand, even in the most insignificant comments and questions. I was always second-guessing myself and others.

"Sure," I accepted.

He began tripping over his words a bit and I could see that he was very nervous and shy, but also very taken with me. So I jumped in and tried to break the ice to help him feel more comfortable. "Can I sit by you?" I asked boldly with growing confidence, sensing his attraction to me.

"Uh . . . sure! Great!" he replied with a smile.

I thought it was very sweet that he was nervous talking to me. From the very beginning of our conversation I could sense he was genuine and sincere—not at all like the smooth-talkers of my past relationships.

After the service, he told me that a lot of the youth group usually went to Hardee's after church to eat and hang out, and he asked, "Do you want to come along?"

I eagerly replied yes. I was excited about the opportunity to spend time with him outside of church and agreed to meet him at the restaurant.

My sister was not at church that evening, so I'd driven alone. During the short drive to the restaurant, I was both nervous and excited. I sensed this could be the beginning of a promising relationship, unlike my past experiences.

As we sat in a booth together, oblivious to the noise and people around us, we began to get to know each other, intently talking. In the course of small talk, he suddenly asked a core question that took me off guard. "What do you want to do with your life?"

I answered by first sharing that I was working full time, and that I was also self-employed in cosmetics. Then I told him I loved fashion and beauty and had a passion to help other women feel good about their natural beauty.

His eyes lit up, and he enthusiastically responded, "I love that entrepreneurship in you," and went on to share that he was a photographer.

We were discovering our compatibility as we continued to get to know each other. We had an increasing and mutual excitement and admiration for each other.

Before the evening was over, he asked me for a date, and of course I agreed! I almost floated out of Hardee's. The shared enthusiasm growing between us was exhilarating and I looked forward to our next meeting with much anticipation.

For our first date, we were planning to eat at a pizza place then have dessert at Dunkin' Donuts. When he picked me up, though, I was surprised to see he wasn't alone. He had invited his best friend to join us. I realized this was his safety net for his nervousness about our first date. I accepted the twist of events, just happy to spend time with him, even though I had wanted to be alone with him. However, I felt flattered that he liked me so much that it made him that nervous.

He had previously shared that he was into photography, but I was surprised to find he'd brought his camera on our date. He said he wanted to take a couple of photos of me. "You'll be great to photograph!" he said enthusiastically. "You're beautiful enough to be a model."

I was very flattered. My heart was so full, but I wasn't prepared for a photo shoot!

His camera in hand, I turned away, feeling unprepared and shy in the sudden spotlight—and with his best friend looking on. Jeff was exuberant, though, and when I turned back around, he snapped my photo! The spontaneity was funny and fun and I began to relax and allowed him to take a few more shots. It was an enjoyable evening.

Our date ended with Jeff walking me to my door (just he and I), and he said, "I want our next date to be just the two of us."

I eagerly agreed, thankful that our next date would be *without* extra company. We stood awkwardly for a moment then he gave me a warm hug with the promise of a phone call.

Our relationship continued to blossom as we saw each other often at church, shared lengthy phone conversations, and dated each other regularly. We were both committed to Christ and both growing more comfortable with the newness and excitement of our building relationship. We were both gaining more confidence around each other as we became closer, spending a lot of time together. We were with each other steadily, almost every weekend. And we talked on the phone throughout the week.

One night, as we were sitting downstairs on my parents' couch, getting ready to watch a movie, I surprised him with my own strange question. "I'm curious," I began, "what were you doing in your life about two months ago?" It had been exactly two months earlier that I had received the prophecy that God was preparing my future husband to come into my life, and that he would be finishing school at Illinois Central College when we met.

His response was chilling! "Oh, I was just finishing up a few courses at ICC."

I was amazed. I then confided to him the prophecy I had received two months before. He was amazed as well and shared that he, too, had been praying that God would bring his future wife to him.

WOW! God is so faithful to hear and answer our prayers!

Interestingly, prior to me sharing the prophecy with him and our shared discovery of each other's individual prayers, we had had several people from church (seven in all) who had said, "You two just go together! You're going to get married."

Each time, we both had just laughed, slightly embarrassed by all the attention we were getting from others. Now we were certain that it was God who had brought us together.

After only three weeks of dating, Jeff proposed; and I said, "Yes!"

We announced our intentions to our parents and, needless to say, they were a bit taken aback. We went on to share bits of our hearts with them and they too felt it was God's hand that had brought the two of us together.

We wanted to use wisdom in making wedding plans, so we set the wedding date for one year later, to give us further time to know each other better.

The months passed quickly and I was ecstatic. Jeff was truly a gentleman. He opened doors for me, showed up at my door with flowers and other gifts, and put love notes on my car window with a rose. I felt like a true princess. I was attracted to him not only physically but also to his integrity and commitment to God, and his respect for me as his future bride. He was attracted to me physically, too; however, his respect for me, in hand with his strong values, caused him to strive to keep our physical relationship pure.

On the other hand, my past relationships with boys had taught me that I was acceptable when I gave myself to them fully—not simply emotionally but also physically. I knew that pursuing Jeff sexually was wrong according to God's principles of purity, but I persisted. The root of rejection, creating an insatiable emotional hunger in me, was still powerfully influencing me to choose ungodly decisions and actions.

Jeff continued to display his love for me in countless Godly ways; but I allowed my deep emotional neediness to drive me to pursue him sexually. Consequently, we entered our marriage impure.

I had tried to forget my past. I had not wanted to remember all the past relationships with guys who had used me and mistreated me, although those experiences had played a large part in shaping how I negatively viewed myself and my worth. I believed the lies about my worth, contrary to how God truly saw me.

I tried to reason away my past by telling myself *that was then, this is now— a new start.* But I had not yet truly changed from the root out, which led to my ungodly choices and behavior patterns. I had wanted to neatly bury those ugly things of my past, never to deal with them again, but that's all I had done—simply masked them instead of digging out the root.

It wasn't until much later in life that I understood I could not get away from my past until I had truly dealt with it *at the root.*

Jeff and I acknowledged to each other, before God, that we had acted outside His perfect will before marriage. The Lord, in His loving kindness, forgave us. Nevertheless, I carried with me into our marriage a lot of unresolved issues which would eventually catch up with me and I'd have to confront.

Jeff and I spent our days enjoying each other's company and reveling in our love. We were happily making our wedding plans. The big day was fast approaching. There were invitations to pick out, the cake and photographer to choose, and, of course, the wedding dress and more. The list went on and on.

Finally our day arrived. We stood before our God, our family, and friends, and pledged our love and vows to each other. What an incredible day!

I told myself, *Surely our wedding day will change everything for the better in me, and surely our wedding will be the dividing line between my past and our future.*

I took confidence in this thought as we went on our honeymoon.

It was bliss! We had a week of sun-filled days on the shores of Myrtle Beach. Our days were filled with fun activities: swimming in the ocean; lounging at the pool; and, of course, plenty of shopping and dining! Each night we held hands and took long walks on the beach to see how many different types of seashells we could find. Everything was perfect as our honeymoon week ended and we headed toward home.

On the long, 2-day drive, we started having some misunderstandings in our communication with each other, and even had an occasional argument. I would easily burst into tears, relentlessly insecure.

Jeff had grown up with two brothers, so he wasn't quite sure how to handle my emotional female outbursts. Of course, I thought he should automatically know what to say to make me feel better, and that he should be filled with unconditional love and understanding.

We continued to have more and more misunderstandings.

I was devastated.

Since God had so obviously picked Jeff and me for each other, I naturally thought things would go smoothly in our relationship. These road bumps were not at all what I'd been expecting. All the while, I wasn't dealing with the deep root of rejection that had long before been festering inside of me. Now it was being fed by misunderstanding and arguments with the man I loved. The arguments we were having were making me more and more insecure in myself.

Unknown to me at the time, Jeff was experiencing his own feelings of rejection. He had grown up the youngest of three boys. His dad was an avid hunter and fisherman and his two older brothers had followed in their dad's footsteps; but not Jeff. At first, Jeff tried to fit into their mold, but hunting and fishing just truly wasn't him. He later confided in me that he felt rejected and unaccepted by them because he did not share their common interests.

I also learned later that he had had only one other serious relationship before ours, which had crushed him. They had had plans to get married, but her father had not approved of

Jeff. Her father was a well-respected executive at a prominent business in our area, and had wanted his daughter to marry someone of similar financial status. She and Jeff had had the wedding rings picked out and were making plans for their future when she abruptly broke up with him, because he would not be able to provide on his current income the substantial financial future she and her family desired; and there was no guarantee of a better job on the horizon.

Jeff's heart was broken.

This major rejection was added to the long-time rejection he had felt from his dad and brothers because he did not share their love for hunting and fishing. His broken heart over the girl he had been planning to marry further rooted in his feelings of rejection and not being "good enough." So, Jeff too carried his own root of rejection from many years into our marriage.

Despairingly, he and I had entered our relationship and marriage with the baggage of deeply wounded hearts that carried deep feelings of rejection and a lack of self-worth. Simply stated, we could not help each other because we could not even help ourselves. We didn't realize at that time how the roots within us were gravely impacting our marriage—right from the start.

The next few years of our life were like a roller coaster ride. Some days we were up— captured with love and passion for each other—and other days we plummeted into heated arguments filled with hurt and miscommunication. Neither of us had dealt with the emotional wounds from our pasts, so they influenced every thought, decision, and action in our relationship. The growing arguments and discord between us was pushing our relationship further and farther apart.

Without realizing it, we were continually watering the root of rejection inside each other. We started doubting that our marriage was from God.

In our humanness and lack of understanding the condition of our hearts, we attempted to fix our problems by treating the symptoms, instead of the root.

In Jeff, thoughts of being inferior and inadequate were temporarily alleviated by putting money in the bank. For me, thoughts of my past and the need to cover my pain were temporarily alleviated by shopping.

Jeff would save money to feel better about him, and I would spend money to feel better about me.

Needless to say, issues surrounding our finances were the most prominent and ongoing arguments we had. Our continually manifesting problems were just *symptoms*, though, of the real problem that we fed: the root of rejection growing stronger in both of us.

Consequently, our marriage continued in a cycle of misunderstandings and arguments for several years, creating a greater and greater distance in our relationship. It seemed like we were on an out-of-control roller coaster ride. We didn't know we were headed for a major crash.

One evening, we got into a terrible argument in our kitchen—one of the worst we had ever had in our 12-year marriage. Looking back, years later, I didn't even remember what we were arguing about, but I well remember that our emotions had quickly heated and escalated, spiraling out of control. As heated words flew, our voices rose with all the hurt and rejection we had both been carrying all those years. It all came spewing out like poisonous venom. We had so much hurt and pain inside us, it culminated in a very painful, ugly, and scary eruption.

Sadly, our children heard the frightening commotion. They had been playing downstairs and came running up, alarmed. They had never heard us so angry and loud with each other.

It was scary for them. They pounded on the kitchen door, pleading for us to let them in. Their little voices were crying, "Mommy! Daddy! What's wrong? Why won't you let us in?"

Jeff and I just stood there, momentarily hushed by their pleading little voices which quickly sobered our yelling. We realized the magnitude of the situation we were in—not only gravely impacting our marriage, but terrifying our children.

Jeff and I had just witnessed the most broken and devastating moment of all our years together. We realized we were in a pit far too deep to pull ourselves out.

We needed help. We needed someone to rescue us from ourselves and the strong roots within us that were squeezing the life out of our relationship and tearing us apart. We needed someone to reach down to us in our darkest hour.

In that moment, we both realized there was nowhere else to turn except to God.

We needed a divine intervention—a miracle—to save, heal, and restore our marriage.

Jeff led by example. He dropped to his knees and with all anguish and raw emotion cried out, "Jesus! Help us! Forgive us! Heal us! Restore our marriage and make it what You want it to be."

I followed and did the same, and we wept in each other's arms with our Savior.

We could still hear our children quietly whimpering outside the door. Jeff let them in and immediately knelt down in front of them. He asked our girls to forgive daddy and mommy for scaring them, and for yelling, and for saying those ugly things to each other. He explained to them that we had also asked Jesus to forgive us and to help our marriage and family to be stronger. He affirmed to our children that we would be together for better and for worse, and that somehow Jesus was going to help us become a stronger family.

We all wept together.

I will never forget that picture in my mind, the five of us clinging to each other in a family hug and loving on each other through our tears. I knew that Jesus—our Prince of Peace—had heard our desperate pleas for help and was in our midst, beginning the rooting-out and healing process.

It had taken Jeff and me coming to the very end of ourselves to step onto the long road of healing, both as individuals, as a couple, and as parents to our precious girls. It had taken us getting everything completely out in the open and pleading for God's forgiveness and healing from all the years of pain and rejection we were both suffering—and unknowingly passing on to the next generation. It was up to us to partner with Christ to break those generational curses.

God is faithful.
He was faithful to keep His promise to us for healing and wholeness.

Hours after that horrifying explosion, I wept as the nightmarish scene replayed in my mind. I wondered how we could have allowed things to get so bad between us. I was still completely broken. My heart felt raw with pain. Yet I also felt a relief that we had finally stopped striving on our own and had truly given our marriage and family back to God. Now, we needed to stay on His path to righteousness and freedom of heart and mind.

It was in those moments of surrendering our life, our marriage, and our family to Him that the Holy Spirit spoke to my heart, "Truly, truly I say to you, unless a grain of wheat falls into the earth and dies, it remains alone; but if it dies, it bears much fruit" (John 12:24).

I knew exactly what He was saying to me. For the first time in our marriage, Jeff and I had truly died to ourselves and to the wrong ways we had dealt with issues in our marriage. Now we were putting our trust in God to help us fix our marriage and bring a good harvest from it.

A seed doesn't blossom overnight.
It takes years of watering and tender care,
with faces to the Son.

So was the case with our marriage. Things didn't appear wonderful overnight.

Love and tenderness were restored, but there needed to be much work poured into ourselves and our relationship. Our problems had not begun overnight, so the issues would not be repaired and restored overnight. But now that all the walls had been broken down, we could begin to rebuild on a new and solid foundation this time: the living and freeing principles of God's Word. That was a beautiful thing.

Our marriage continued to grow and flourish as we continued to water and nurture with Christ the seeds of restored love which were in our hearts, while keeping our eyes on our heavenly Father.

Naturally, we had an occasional argument, but we were determined to work things out *God's way*. We practiced openly and honestly discussing our issues to get to the real *root*, instead of simply covering them up and allowing bad and hurtful feelings to further feed the ugly roots. We were now determined to destroy the roots of rejection.

This was the beginning of a wonderful new journey for us, but it would be met with thc challenges and hardships that this life naturally brings.

God continued to grow and strengthen our marriage as we looked to Him and His Word for guidance. We chose to take the hard road and really work through our issues by looking honestly and openly at our individual past hurts to see how they were impacting—and even creating—the present issues between us. We began to experience a freedom in our marriage we had never known before. And to this day, God continues to bless our marriage as we follow His principles and "take delight in the Lord" (Psalm 37:4 NIV).

God truly can breathe upon something that was dead and broken and give it new life.
He can make a way in the wilderness where there seems to be no way.

As it turned out, my heavenly Father had truly gifted me, His daughter, with a wonderful, loving, Godly husband—just as I had asked Him for so many years before.

"You are from God, little children, and have overcome them; because greater is He who is in you than he who is in the world."
1 John 4:4

Chapter 3

Freedom from the Opinions of Others

As the months passed, Jeff and I continued to grow stronger in our marriage and in our relationship with the Lord—together. God was really doing a deep work in us, knitting us together in heart and spirit. We were starting to walk in an increased unity we had not experienced previously in our marriage. The Lord was continuing to build on the new foundation of our marriage that was laid that day we'd chosen to die to our old ways and committed ourselves individually and as a couple to living life God's way.

This newfound unity was a core building block, one of the first things God used to strengthen and help build our marriage on Him—the solid rock. This was the beginning of a wonderfully freeing, but not-so-easy, new journey for us. We were becoming "one" with Christ.

"For this reason a man shall leave his father and his mother,
and be joined ["cleave" KJV] to his wife;
and they shall become one flesh."
Genesis 2:24

Until the "new birth" of our marriage, I had never really given this scripture much thought, nor had I fully understood it. The Lord began to reveal His heart to both Jeff and me about the importance of cleaving (clinging) to each other.

In the earlier years of our marriage, until that turning point when we had invited Christ into our marriage, I was still very attached to my extended family: my dad, mom, and sister. I learned that there's a difference between having a close relationship with your family after marriage and still "cleaving" to them instead of to your husband. I thought my cleaving attachment to my family was completely normal. It didn't appear to me at the time how out-of-balance or unhealthy my clinging attachment to them was—even though on more than one occasion Jeff had told me he felt more like my live-in boyfriend than my husband.

God's truth is this: When Jeff and I married we became our own family unit, independent from our now-extended families.

Without even realizing it, I had continued to take my problems, concerns, and advice-seeking to my family first, instead of to my husband. Consequently, the early years of our marriage had remained somewhat stagnant, though ignited with arguments. We had not experienced the true joy or fulfillment of being "one" as God intended. I had been blinded to the fact that my husband was only getting *part* of me.

The Lord began to challenge my thinking and show me His heart for our marriage: unity and growth with Jeff. Our marriage relationship had, in part, gotten so far out of balance because of my choices to remain emotionally dependent on my dad, mom, sister, and friends, instead of dependent on who God had created me to be as an individual and in partnership with Jeff.

Jeff and I saw that growing together as "one" would require us to make some new and radical changes. For a season, we chose to largely withdraw from my extended family and close friends. I sensed in both that our drastic change was somewhat extreme, like the pendulum of a clock swinging to the other side. But Jeff and I felt the extreme was necessary for a time, so we could truly have opportunity to become rooted in our marriage relationship together—as one.

However, while this change was needed, it prompted that ugly root of rejection to rise higher in me. I was still so drawn to want to please *everyone* in my life, out of my still-rooted insecurities and need for acceptance. I was still greatly influenced by others' thoughts and opinions of my choices. But trying to please everyone (which was impossible in itself) would be at the cost of doing the right thing: being firmly rooted in God's principle of oneness in our marriage, united together with God above all others.

For years I had been in bondage to other people's thoughts and opinions of me and my decisions. My desire to please everyone was greatly influenced by what I perceived (and sometimes knew for a fact) others were thinking, negatively. I was most especially sensitive to the thoughts and feelings of my dad, mom, and sister. I loved them each deeply, but as a grown and married woman I too often allowed their feelings and opinions to control my decisions. I didn't want *anyone* to reject me or be unhappy with me; it was just too painful. But it was also impossible to please everyone, and wrong of me to strive for this above God and Jeff and the individual God had created me to be as a free and empowered woman of faith.

Change was needed.

I desperately needed to get my relational priorities in order. I needed to put God first above all others, then Jeff and our children—our own family unit. Not only did I need to make new changes with my relationship priorities, but also with my consuming emotional need to please people and be influenced by their thoughts and expressed feelings. I needed to practice Romans 12:2 (NIV):

"Be transformed by the renewing of your mind."

And I needed to do this God's way:

"*. . . take captive every thought to make it obedient to Christ.*"
2 Corinthians 10:5 (NIV)

I began to make a conscious choice with every circumstance to take captive every thought. For the sake of my relationship with God, my marriage relationship with Jeff, and our growing family, that stubborn and debilitating root of rejection within me needed to be dug out—one thought at a time.

Choosing God's way was beginning to make me FREE.

Part of my newfound freedom was in God showing me that I didn't owe extended family members and friends an explanation for the decisions I made for myself—a grown and married woman and mother. Nor did Jeff and I owe anyone an explanation for the decisions we made for our marriage and our family.

A prime example of me striving to please others was in regard to answering my telephone.

I used to be somewhat of a slave to answering phone calls. Whenever the phone rang, I felt I had to answer it. Honestly, I didn't really even enjoy talking on the phone. Yet, whenever it rang, that "pleasing others" root of insecurity inside me caused me to believe it was my duty or obligation to answer. Like a servant being summoned by a bell, I was a slave to answering to others.

We cannot strive to fully please God
and man at the same time.
This will only leave us frustrated and depleted of energy.

One day it occurred to me that I had CHOICES! Wow! How freeing it was for me to understand that I didn't have to answer my phone when it rang. I had the *choice* to let my answering machine take the calls whenever it wasn't a good time for me to talk. (At that time the "answering machine" was common, rather than the now-popular voice mail.) And I had the freedom to return the calls in the timeframe best for me and my family. This realization of personal choices (which God has gifted to each of us) was truly life-changing—*freeing*—for me.

Naturally, though, our choices impact others. Not always in a positive way.

I sensed frustration and annoyance from those who were used to me answering the phone whenever they called. Even though the Lord was showing me how to bring His freedom and balance into my life, the old root of rejection in me (not yet completely dug out) continued to try to influence the thoughts I was striving to take captive.

There's always a dichotomy, a tug-of-war, in the process of change. It's not easy to break old patterns and habits.

I loved the freedom from self-slavery I was experiencing by enforcing my freedom of personal choices, yet the feeling of rejection regarding others would try to trap me again and again. This is where the daily, hourly, situation-by-situation practice of 2 Corinthians 10:5 and Romans 12:2 came into play. I had to consciously practice letting go of those enslaving thoughts and opinions of people by consistently speaking God's *truths* to myself.

In Him we find *freedom.*

As time went on, the Lord also began to free me from the need to constantly give explanations to people for the choices I was making, and oftentimes for the direction I sensed the Lord was leading me. His Word says, "The fear of man brings a snare, but he who trusts in the Lord will be exalted" (Proverbs 29:25).

Like the telephone, and giving explanations for my decisions, I was also a slave to being perfect.

For years, I was so consumed with the thoughts and opinions of others that it drove me to be performance-oriented in my behaviors. I felt I had to be *perfect* in everything I did. Perfect looking, perfect marriage, perfect children, perfect house . . . This mindset kept me from experiencing true intimacy with the Lord and the freedom to be "me" which He offers. Again, I needed to make different choices, and God provided many opportunities.

While the deeply-rooted issues I carried was a gradual process of perseverance to change, I began to see the strength of character and enduring confidence God was growing in me toward becoming who He had created and desired me to be: a confident, Spirit-empowered and Spirit-led, free of heart and mind, woman of God.

"We also exult in our tribulations,
knowing that tribulation brings about perseverance;
and perseverance, proven character;
and proven character, hope; and hope does
not disappoint, because the love of God
has been poured out within our hearts
through the Holy Spirit who was given to us."
Romans 5:3-5

"Self" dies in the wilderness.

Changes which need to take place within us for our betterment often happen during those spiritual desert seasons that God allows, and sometimes even leads us into for our growth. Had it not been for the wilderness seasons in my life, I don't believe I would have died to my old self and grown stronger in character and confidence in Christ.

As I began to experience true intimacy with Christ, He cultivated a strong desire in me to seek Him, know Him and His Word, and obey His will for my life above all else. Slowly but surely, the thoughts and opinions of others became a far less driving force as I allowed His power to root out the feelings of rejection, and His love and truths to grow in its place. Once I no longer allowed myself to be limited or controlled by my self-focused thoughts concerning others, His purposes and plans were able to be fulfilled in and through me.

It's amazing to me, though, how opposition and testing grow stronger when we decide to give our lives fully and completely to Christ by living in radical obedience to Him.

The evil one, Satan, doesn't work so hard in our lives when we're not following Christ. But when we turn against sin and evil by fully turning to Christ—listening to God's Spirit within us and following the principles of His Word—Satan is stirred up against us! He works overtime to trip us up and wear us down in the hope that we'll give up!

"For our struggle is not against flesh and blood, but against the rulers, against the powers,
against the world forces of this darkness, against the spiritual forces of wickedness in the heavenly places."
Ephesians 6:12

It also amazes me that the evil one uses people against us when we boldly and uncompromisingly begin to speak about the personal freedom we're gaining in Christ, and the bondages He is releasing us from.

As I grew in Christ, I experienced times when people close to me, outside our immediate family unit, were uncomfortable with the "new me," and even spoke out against me in judgment. Their rejection of me *hurt* and served to further feed that ugly root I was working with Christ to dig out. It was truly painful to be rejected by those close to me when I knew without a doubt that I was giving 100 percent to following God's direction, by practicing the principles of His Word and striving to live according to His purpose for me.

Through perseverance with Christ, I gained a greater strength to stand on what I believed He was instructing me to do in any given circumstance, and was determined to no longer allow the negative opinions and judgments of others to rule over me.

It was a painful process, but in the end it brought needed death of my self-centered focus and freedom from the root of rejection regarding others. Following Christ allowed me to more fully know, experience, and take great delight in sensing His favor, love, and pleasure over my obedience to Him. I was striving wholeheartedly to live as His Word tells us to live: "Seek first His kingdom and His righteousness . . . " (Matthew 6:33).

As I put God first, above people, I began to see that He would take care of other people's thoughts and judgments. I didn't need to worry about or focus on those as "worries" because He promised to take care of *all* my needs when I sought His kingdom and His righteousness first. (Matthew 6:31-34)

I was gradually becoming free from the root of rejection and learning to step out in faith to walk in the full destiny of who God had created me to be. And I gained an understanding of Matthew 10:37-40. This passage had confused and concerned me for years. I had believed it was radical and extreme:

> *He who loves father or mother more than Me is not worthy of Me;*
> *and he who loves son or daughter more than Me is not worthy of Me.*
> *And he who does not take his cross and follow after Me is not worthy of Me.*
> *He who has found his life will lose it, and he who has lost his life*
> *for My sake will find it. He who receives you receives Me,*
> *and he who receives Me receives Him who sent Me.*

Because I couldn't comprehend this passage, I would just gloss over it, thinking, *surely God doesn't mean that literally.* But through my journey with Christ and the testing of His principles, I discovered that God's Word is absolute truth! Not in part but in whole. As our Creator, He does, in fact, want us to love Him above all people and give Him first place and priority above all things and all others in our lives—even those we love the most.

This scripture may seem to you as radical and extreme as it did to me before the Lord began to challenge my thinking, to better know and understand who He is: our Creator, GOD, the One who gave His only Son for our eternal salvation; our Father who loves us beyond our understanding and who supplies ALL our needs; the One who makes us free to be who He uniquely designed us each to be as individuals.

While I love my family very much and desire to honor them, I came to understand that there is *no one* who can complete me and free me except God, through Jesus Christ.

Giving my heart, my life, and my love to Christ above all people and things would not only free me to be all He purposed me to be but also enable me to love others as He loves me.

In reality, I had not *rejected* those I loved, but had begun to release myself from all contrary thoughts and opinions which I had carried for so long. I favored following Jesus wholeheartedly and uncompromisingly above all others. And I favored being *one* with Jeff and placing our family values and needs above the thoughts and opinions of others.

I'm reminded of the scripture where Jesus said to the rich man, "If you wish to be *complete*, go and sell your possessions and give to the poor, and you will have treasure in heaven; and come, follow Me" (Matthew 19:21; author's emphasis).

The rich man wept because he had many earthly possessions which were valuable to him. He loved his earthly treasures too much to be willing to forsake them and follow Christ.

The reality of life with Christ is that when we're truly willing to forsake *all* for Him, God gives back to us ". . . far more abundantly beyond all that we ask or think, according to the power that works within us" (Ephesians 3:20).

God will put His finger on the very issues of our hearts that we choose to put above Him. Everything we place above Him in life is in danger of becoming an "idol"—the things and people we love more than we love and honor God.

My idols, in this sense, were my relationships and my perception of how people were judging me—who they thought I should be and what choices I should make. I was constantly striving for the favor and acceptance of people over God's divinely powerful favor. Placing Him first in all things, and above all others, proved to give me a greater Christ-like love and honor for others—and for myself—in every way.

Out of His great love for me, and for the sake of His purposes for me, God used my feelings of rejection and lack of support from people close to me to prune off loving them more than Him. As painful as the pruning process was, it resulted in such a greater freedom for me, and produced greater fruit in me which I could extend to others.

What we give to others from God, rather than from "self" motives,
can offer to them a greater freedom in Christ
and the fullness of God.

In the pruning process He proved another promise from His Word:

"We know that in all things God works
for the good of those who love him,
who have been called according to his purpose."
Romans 8:28 (NIV)

I now know that God's thoughts about me, His direction for me, and pleasing Him above myself and others, is truly what matters *most* in this life. I was growing more free and unrestrained to wholeheartedly follow Jesus wherever He was leading me, even if down roads less traveled or not popular. My desire above all else was to follow Him.

The root of rejection was beginning to burn up under the brilliant Son and transforming power of God's glory. I could truly say that His opinion of me was all that really mattered. This was true *freedom*.

Chapter 4

Finding Your True Identity in Christ

The work that God had done in me (and continues to complete), freeing me from the thoughts and opinions of people, was laying the ground work for the next major building block He was setting into place. He began to challenge me and teach me that my true identity can *only* be found in Jesus Christ—not in the many earthly things I had looked to in the past. The list was long (and very tiresome): how I looked and tried to behave to please others; how my children looked and how they behaved; how our marriage appeared; the money we earned; the house we lived in . . .

I was guilty of putting my identity in *things*, instead of in Christ. A biggie for me was my kids. I believed that how my children looked and behaved was a reflection of me. To a certain extent it is, but it's not the root source of my identity.

One day, my girls and I were seated in a booth across from the soda fountain in Hardee's, having lunch with my grandma. While she and I were talking, my daughters got up to refill their drinks. They were giggling while standing next to the soda fountain.

That was pretty much the extent of it when, out of the blue, an elderly man came over to our table and lit into me about how my children were being a disgrace by wasting Hardee's soda. (Evidently, my girls had put a little soda in their cups then poured it down the drain of the machine.)

I was stunned the whole time he was confronting me because my children were truly not being loud or disruptive, and I wasn't aware they were "wasting" soda. They could have accidentally gotten the wrong type of soda and dumped it out to get another, or had simply overfilled a cup.

He continued his tirade by asking what kind of a mother I was to let my children do such things, and eluded that they were horrible children. Meanwhile, my oldest daughter (who was very sensitive) began to well up with tears. I was shocked at the man's rudeness. I could hardly gather my thoughts to respond, though I managed to tell him I would deal with the situation and curtly told him, "Thank you for informing me."

Inside, I was livid at the way he'd spoken to me, the things he'd said against my children, and how he'd spoken so harshly right in front of them. Clearly he was carrying a big chip on his shoulder. There was an underlying root problem that was festering in him and prompting his outburst—other than a couple of giggling, carefree girls standing by a soda machine.

As we walked to the van, my girls were clearly upset—as I was. One told me she felt sick to her stomach and asked if she was a "bad kid," as that man had called her. I assured her that he was out of line, and that while we needed to respect people's property and have good manners, the way he'd reacted had been wrong. As she continued to cry, I felt distraught seeing my precious daughter so badly shaken up by a stranger's unnecessary outburst, and distraught at being told I was a bad mother for not watching my kids.

To complicate matters further, my grandma (whom I loved dearly and who could be pretty feisty) confronted me on how I should have given him a piece of my mind. She asked me how I could have allowed that man to speak to me and my girls that way. She carried on, saying how she should have "put that old, grumpy man in his place."

After listening to her ranting I replied, "Grandma, I need to be an example to my girls. Yes, you're right; he was out of line in how he spoke to us. But for me to respond on that level, by raising my voice and saying hurtful things back to him, would have been no better than his poor behavior."

Jesus says in Matthew 5:39, "But I say to you, do not resist an evil person; but whoever slaps you on your right cheek, turn the other to him also."

I think my grandma was a little surprised by my response to her; but she saw the truth in it.

After she and I said our goodbyes and it was just my girls and me alone in the van, I had a heart-to-heart talk with them. I explained that our *true* identity is in Jesus Christ, not in what people think or say about us or to us. By example, I explained that our identity is not found in what that man thought of us, or how he'd treated us. I also shared what God says about us, that we're fearfully and wonderfully made.

The full passage from Psalm 139:13-16 is profound to our identity in Christ:

For you formed my inward parts;
You wove me in my mother's womb.
I will give thanks to You, I am fearfully
and wonderfully made; wonderful are Your works,
and my soul knows it very well. My frame was not hidden from You,
when I was made in secret,
and skillfully wrought in the depths of the earth; Your eyes have seen my
unformed substance;
and in Your book were all written the days that
were ordained for me,
when as yet there was not one of them.

"Really Mama?" one responded with relief. "We're not bad girls like he said?" I reiterated to them God's truths about them; but my heart pained again as I realized how easily the root of rejection could be planted in my children's hearts, allowing the generational curse to continue. I was determined that the curse would end there, with my own healing, and not be carried into the next generations. Oh, the damage that carelessly uttered words can do! The truth is spoken clearly in Proverbs 18:21: "Death and life are in the power of the tongue, And those who love it will eat its fruit."

I took time to sit and pray with my girls before we even left the parking lot. My responsibility as a mother, in hand with my own work toward personal healing, was to lay a solid foundation of truth in their hearts: they are important and valuable in the eyes of God; they are important and valuable in my eyes and in their dad's; and God has a distinctive purpose for each of their lives.

As I continued to speak words of truth and life into my daughters, I could see their confidence growing. I was thankful God had helped me to have self-control and make the right choice in my response to the angry stranger by not rising up in anger myself to defend us (as I wanted to do in my human nature).

When we're rooted and grounded in the truth
that our true identity lies in Christ
—and Him alone—
we will remain unshaken in diverse and difficult circumstances.

Weeks later, when my mom came to visit, we were standing in the back yard while the kids played on their swing set. I went into the garage to get a couple of chairs so we could sit outside in view of the girls. I immediately noticed how our cheap plastic chairs were bleached out from the sun, and how dirty and cracked they were. I offered my mom a chair and felt somewhat ashamed that they were in such bad condition.

Trying to put my worth in *things* (rather than in Christ), robs my peace and joy. I could have *taken captive every thought* by choosing to have a positive attitude about the chairs, thinking about how thankful we were to have chairs and a nice, fenced-in backyard with a swing set, but I had focused on my aging chairs instead.

Once I got my mind on something negative, a domino effect would take place. Other truly unimportant "things" that were wearing on me would surface and stand out in my mind: the over-grown weeds; the rust on the fence . . . The negative list would grow and consume my mind, not leaving room to think on the many blessings we had, and on my mom who had come to visit. I was putting my identity (my worth) in material things and not in what truly matters: my relationship with Jesus and with those I love.

Earthly things will pass away; they are temporary. But Jesus and those He has entrusted to us to love and care for are *eternal.* It's a waste of time and will wear us down when we allow our minds to be captivated by material possessions, and trying to keep up with the material wealth we may see in our neighbors.

In our society, there's so much pressure to "keep up with the Joneses"—having the nicest house, vehicles, the latest technology . . . If we're not careful, we can too quickly fall into this trap which focuses our vision on temporary things that truly will not matter at all in the end, instead of focusing on our relationship with Christ and loving our neighbors as ourselves. (Matthew 19:19)

God continued to establish these truths in me.

It's a process to
"Be transformed by the renewing of your mind."
Romans 12:2 (NIV)

There was a continual warring inside me, a continual choice in what—and in whom—I was going to place my identity.

God's Word says we are to ". . . take captive every thought to make it obedient to Christ" (2 Corinthians 10:5 NIV).

Therefore, I had to daily work at rooting out my old way of thinking (taking captive my every thought) and begin to embrace God's truths in my mind.

God would continue a pruning process in me, removing material things I held dear to refocus my thoughts on eternal things: my husband, our relationship, our children, extended family and friends—people—whom I could encourage in Christ.

"Things" (and others) can easily become "idols" in our lives.

Our financial situation was very tight. It seemed we were having trouble making ends meet with every paycheck. Taking a serious look at our income and expenses, Jeff came to the decision that we should get rid of our cell phone, believing this expense was not really a necessity. I had such a hard time with that decision. *Everyone has a cell phone*, I told myself. *I can't believe we have to get rid of ours!*

I was having my own little pity party over the thought of letting go of my cell phone. Not only did having a cell phone make me feel as though I fit in with what appeared to be normal day-to-day life around me, but it was, in truth, a convenience which made life a little easier. For the sake of our own financial needs, though, I conceded that I could live without a cell phone. I knew Jeff was right. I knew it was best for our finances to get rid of that expense; but I was resentful. I wanted to fit in with our society.

Looking back, I saw that the root of my desire had less to do with whether or not my cell phone was truly needed and more to do with how I looked to others, how they might view me, and how I felt about myself. I felt "lower grade" without a cell phone. It had become a normal part of everyday life in our culture (and for me) and I wanted to "fit in"—just like I had wanted to fit in with the "cool" kids in junior high and high school.

Through these experiences and my willingness to look at myself in light of God's truths, I began to grow further in the knowledge that my *true* identity is not found in material things or status, or how people may view me. My true identity is only found in the One who gave me life and lives inside me: God and His indwelling Spirit through Jesus Christ.

As a result of surrendering to God's truths, His ways, and His perfect timing, He often gives back to us the things we desire but don't necessarily need. As a loving and generous Father, He desires to give us good gifts. (Ephesians 3:20) He also desires that we be emotionally and spiritually mature enough to use those gifts responsibly, and with *right motives.*

About two years (and a lot of personal growth) later, I was able to get a cell phone again, but the status of having a cell phone was no longer the driving force. I truly appreciated the blessing and convenience it offered.

God looks at our hearts and motives in all things.

"God sees not as man sees, for man looks at the
outward appearance,
but the Lord looks at the heart."
1 Samuel 16:7

Often I have to stop and ask myself, *Why am I doing this? What is my motive?*—even when it comes my appearance.

My identity was strongly tied to how I looked on the outside. For example, the clothes I wore.

For years, I felt the urge to buy a new shirt or outfit about every two weeks. There was a short-term excitement and joy in having something new to wear; but it was truly short-lived. I still had an emotional hunger for approval and acceptance from others that shopping and looking nice couldn't fill. It was a black void of internal emptiness that was only temporarily satisfied when I put on something new.

While my family was struggling financially, I had plenty of nice, fashionable clothes in my closet. Shopping at the expense of the true needs of our family had grown to become an emotional "fix" I craved like a drug. I would feel an urge, a driving force, to buy something new. Instead of shopping with my head, I shopped with my emotions—my neediness to feel better about myself and the void inside me.

While I had the desire to look nice, I also had a growing desire to be 'new' on the inside. I wanted to become the whole and Godly woman I knew God wanted me to be.

As I continued to look inside myself, I began to realize that my need to shop was never going to complete me on the inside. Only God could do that. I needed to allow Him to clothe me on the inside, where I was really naked and destitute for everlasting clothing. I realized that I was not only being a poor steward of my husband's hard-earned salary, but a poor steward of the priceless value and worth God had already placed on me, simply because I was His creation, His daughter, His heir.

While I was worrying about the way I looked on the outside, God was most concerned about completing me on the inside. He says in Matthew 6:28-30:

> *"And why are you worried about clothing?*
> *Observe how the lilies of the field grow;*
> *they do not toil nor do they spin,*
> *yet I say to you that not even Solomon in all his glory*
> *clothed himself like one of these.*
> *But if God so clothes the grass of the field,*
> *which is alive today and tomorrow*
> *thrown into the furnace, will He not much more clothe you?"*

God's clothing is eternally satisfying. Once clothed in His righteousness, there's no longer an addiction for things that are temporary—"here today and tomorrow is thrown into the furnace."

I began to see through the light of His Word that I had been putting my root identity in clothes and in my overall outward appearance instead of in Him.

Now, I was *still* a prissy, fashion-loving woman (as I am today), but my perspective had changed (instead of my closet). I was beginning to understand that loving beautiful things is not wrong or bad, but I couldn't allow the temporary things of this world to control or define me, nor would they ever complete me.

I began to control the buying instead of the buying controlling me.

I was beginning to understand how truly valuable I am in Christ and that my identity and worth is not in the clothes I wear or how I look. It's in His garment of righteousness and the truth that He loves and accepts me just as I am.

⁂

When Jeff and I first got married, he worked at a very small shop and was earning a very meager wage. I worked part time and didn't make much over minimum wage. There was a time when I was so bothered by the meager yearly income we brought home, I was mortified at the thought of anyone finding out. All the while, we never lacked a thing we truly needed.

We had a cute mobile home that was very nice, fully equipped with everything we needed. Yet, there was a part of me that felt inferior to those who had nicer, bigger homes, and a larger income. Again, I was putting my identity in the wrong things—temporary things.

I believe my misplaced identity stemmed from the root of rejection I was carrying. I had bought into the lie that if I had nice things, and we made more money, we would be more accepted by those around us. This lie is from the enemy of our souls.

There's a song I like called *The Measure of a Man.* It talks about the true worth of an individual not being found in how wealthy or intelligent he or she is, but rather in the heart. It's true. There's so much more to life than trying to attain riches.

The Bible tells us, "Do not store up for yourselves treasures on earth . . . But store up for yourselves treasures in heaven, where neither moth nor rust destroys, and where thieves do not break in or steal; for where your treasure is, there your heart will be also"(Matthew 6:19-21).

Again, it's not wrong to have nice things and like nice things. I certainly enjoy nice things! It's rather a matter of our hearts, our motives—why we want the things we want and if those things are of higher importance than things of *eternal value*.

Do we own earthy things or do our earthy things own us?

I liked my husband's quote: "It's all going to burn in the end!"

God sometimes gently reminds me of this when I get too worked up over material things.

When we got Lacey, our Golden Retriever, my biggest fear was that she was going to take a hunk out of my precious furniture. I really prided myself on how nice our furniture looked. We had spent quite a bit to purchase the pieces and worked to keep them "like new." So I usually watched Lacey like a hawk when she was in the living room. Under my watchful eye she would do no damage.

One morning, my youngest daughter, Karissa, was in the living room watching cartoons. I was in my bedroom talking on the phone to a close friend who lived out of state. For once, I had left the dog alone in the living room. I had checked on her just a few minutes before the call and she'd been lying on our hardwood floor, happily chewing on a bone. Talking on the phone for only ten minutes, I was sure I would walk out to find her still on the floor and Karissa still watching cartoons in the chair. I was feeling kind of proud of myself for my new laid-back attitude. *See*, I told myself, *you've been too uptight about the dog. You can turn your back on her for ten minutes without her destroying something.*

I walked into the living room and to my dismay found Lacy sitting in the chair with my daughter, who was crying and trying with all her 4-year-old might to cover the arm of my precious La-Z-Boy.

My stomach dropped.

"What happened?" I yelled at my daughter, despite the tears in her big blues!

"I don't want to show you, Mommy," she cried, her little hand still grasped firmly in place, covering the arm of my chair. She knew the dog was not allowed on "Mommy's furniture."

Finally I saw that the more I ranted and raved, the more upset my little girl became. The yelling was getting me nowhere, and I was upset at *myself* for causing my precious young daughter to cry.

I pushed aside my thoughts of the possibly damaged chair in favor of my possibly damaged daughter. "It's okay, sweetie; just let Mommy see."

What a difference it makes when we're calm in our dealings with people rather than blowing up over truly unimportant things. (I would try to remember that in the future.)

"Are you sure if I show you, Mommy, I won't be in trouble?" Karissa asked tentatively.

I felt so bad for how worked up I had become to cause my innocent child so much unnecessary turmoil. I assured her, "It'll be okay, baby; Mommy isn't mad at you and I'm sorry." At this, she cried even more but moved her hand so I could assess the damage.

Lacey had, in fact, chewed a hole in the chair arm's sleeve cover, but not the arm itself. I was a little upset that I no longer had matching sleeve covers for our La-Z-Boy, but more upset with myself for choosing to put my possessions above my child's feelings. She was, after all, four years old and not the one responsible for the dog. I was the mom; I was responsible for the dog *and* for the way I behaved with my children. If the puppy had decided to jump up on her lap while she watched her favorite show, it was unfair for me to scold her unnecessarily.

I learned a valuable lesson that day: earthly things can be replaced, but people cannot. Earthly things can be mended, but a person's bruised or broken heart, or torn mind, not so easily.

When harsh, angry words are spoken in the heat of the moment, we instill damage in others. By God's grace, I would be working to make sure I valued people and relationships more than worldly treasures, just as God values me more than anything in this life.

As we place our true identity in the Lord, we are better able to love and value people as God does, and intends for us to do.

For most of my life, I lacked any real sense of identity—not only during my childhood years but also into my early adult years. It wasn't until my thirties that I discovered my true identity in Christ as a child of God.

It's natural for children to look to their parents (especially to their dads) to speak identity, value, and worth into their lives—which is a reflection and demonstration of God's love and value for us. We find an example of this in Genesis 27:38.

Esau confronted his father, Isaac, about the blessing Isaac spoke over his younger brother Jacob. Esau said to his father, "Do you have only one blessing, my father? Bless me, even me also, O my father." Esau lifted his voice and wept with his desire for his father's blessing.

Through this passage we feel Esau's raw desire, pain, and bitterness of soul, because he longed for his father's blessing and wasn't receiving it. This is sadly the case for many young people and adults today. The longing within us for our parents' blessing, if not received, leaves a great void.

There's a desire in each of us for the blessing of our parents and for them to call out the gold in us. When our parents speak words of blessing, direction, and affirmation into our lives, day in and day out, it builds in us the truth of our worth and value. It prepares us to grow into the person God created us to be for specific purposes; and it points to the One who completes us and satisfies our spirits at the root: God the Father through His Son, Jesus Christ.

It's been God's design from the beginning of time for parents to speak blessings over their children, and this is His design and expectation for parents today.

Jacob went to such extreme measures to get his father's blessings that he ended up deceiving his father into believing he was his brother Esau.

In Bible times, a father's blessing was greatly sought after. A father's blessing was powerful because it carried privilege, position, and supremacy in the family, and a double portion of the inheritance—all of which served as a reflection of God as our heavenly Father.

While supremacy in the family or a double portion of the inheritance may not be the case today, the emotional need and desire is still the same in every individual.

Throughout the new covenant (the New Testament), God has given parents a mandate, a high calling to bless, affirm, mentor, and speak identity into the lives of their children, giving their time, teaching, and mentoring; pouring into their children worth and value on a daily basis through countless acts of love and service.

I believe one of the primary reasons there are so many teen pregnancies, violence, and countless other ungodly behaviors, is due to the lack of parents walking alongside their children daily, giving their love through their time, teaching, and mentoring; pouring into their children unconditional love, grace, mercy . . . all the fruit of the Spirit. (Galatians 5:22-23)

By putting aside our own selfish desires as parents, to invest in our children's emotional, mental, physical, and spiritual needs on a daily basis, we're sowing not only into their lives but also into future generations. When we choose to invest in our children's core needs and well-being, we're sowing into, and building up, their identity—their worth and value—in Christ, which they in turn will sow into their own children. At the same time, we are also rooting out generational curses that lead to crisis of identity in our young people.

When we invest in our children's spirits, we are investing in things of generational and eternal value, applying Proverbs 22:6:

"Train up a child in the way he should go,
even when he is old [mature] he will not depart from it."

By following this command, we are building up and passing on a Godly legacy, storing up blessings for our children and future generations. In turn, our children will grow up to teach, mentor, care for, and train up their own children in God's ways by what they have learned from us and witnessed in our behaviors as parents.

"He will restore the hearts of the fathers to their children
and the hearts of the children to their fathers."
Malachi 4:6

I believe we're living in a time when we're going to see this prophecy fulfilled on a greater level than ever before.

God continues to remind Jeff and me of the mandate, and awesome privilege and responsibility, to pour into, train up, and selflessly love and speak Christ's fullness and wholeness into our children's lives. He has challenged us to stop focusing so much on our own selfish desires (which are of little value), in favor of concentrating on being actively involved in our daughters' lives, teaching them their true identity in Christ rather than in the temporary, unfulfilling things of this life.

Amazingly, as Jeff and I began this process, we too began to learn that no matter what our own childhood experiences were, our true identity and worth is found in Jesus Christ. By partnering with Him to practice the truths of His Word we can fulfill His purposes for our lives while also investing in what He sees as valuable and eternal.

Chapter 5

Establishing Boundaries: A New Normal

After becoming more rooted and grounded in my new identity in Christ, I, along with Jeff, began to establish healthier relationship boundaries with others. I like to refer to this as "the new normal."

Relationships with others had been so vastly out of balance for us for too many years. We had some serious changes that needed to take place.

Previous to that realization and learning my true identity in Christ, I had allowed people to talk down to me, meanly tease me, and take advantage of me. I had not set healthy boundaries which would protect me, Jeff, our marriage, our family, or our home. Our home had not felt like a true haven for me or my family.

When our second child was born, we outgrew our mobile home and were blessed to be able to move into a house, giving us more space. Jeff's dad had been retiring at the time and he and Jeff's mom wanted to relocate to Missouri. We were blessed to be able to purchase their home.

I was ecstatic to be leaving our tiny mobile home to move into a 3-bedroom ranch, complete with a full basement and 2 bathrooms. We were so thankful for this opportunity and blessing; however, we were unprepared for the intrusive encounters we would soon face from the very first day we moved in.

Our neighbors, Sally and her husband John, were parents of two girls who had moved into the neighborhood years ago, at the same time Jeff's parents had. Jeff and his brothers were close in age to the two neighboring girls. The timing of two families moving into the neighborhood, both with children near the same age, prompted Jeff's mom and Sally to become fast friends. They connected immediately from day one.

The closeness of their quickly-growing relationship extended to allowing Sally the freedom to walk into Jeff's parents' home at will, unannounced, without knocking or ringing the doorbell. And both Sally and John grew accustomed to coming into Jeff's parents' yard at will to sit and visit. No healthy boundaries of property or family privacy were set. The lack of healthy (and normally expected) boundaries produced deeply rooted behaviors of disrespect that were allowed to continue over the course of many years.

By nature, Jeff's mom was a laid-back woman. She and Sally had become such close friends so quickly; perhaps the disregard for privacy boundaries had been perfectly acceptable to Jeff's mom. Consequently, Jeff grew up accustomed to Sally appearing in his house unannounced as she pleased. As well, Sally and John freely made themselves at home in Jeff's backyard whenever his parents were outside.

I had met Sally when Jeff and I were dating and had witnessed a number of occasions when she'd just pop in without knocking. This felt very intrusive to me, abnormal and uncomfortable, because I had not grown up this way—nor had ever known anyone who had, until I met Jeff. I was accustomed to the normal common courtesy of friends and relatives calling before coming to visit, and most certainly knocking on the door or ringing the doorbell, then waiting to be invited in—or not.

Jeff's parents had moved to another state and we had become the "new family" in the neighborhood, moving into our own home. So, I was unprepared and stunned when on our very first day, Sally just walked right into our home like it was her own. I was not simply surprised; I was shocked, then angry. But I felt too timid to say anything to her about it. I was too afraid of Sally's possible rejection of me if I set boundaries with her. It was our first day in our new home, with new neighbors, and I was afraid of possibly hurting her feelings.

The root of rejection in me had grown very deep by the time Jeff and I married.

It was that first day in our new home that I realized how accustomed Sally was to entering the house as she pleased, without a second thought; but I didn't consider that this abnormal behavior would *continue*. After all, we were not Jeff's parents and it was no longer their home, and we had not yet established any kind of adult relationship with Sally and John.

Sadly, our exciting first day in our new home would prove to be the beginning of a continual invasion of our family's privacy for many years to come.

Jeff was used to Sally's intrusions. He'd grown up with her and John's familiarity in his home and yard, but I had not. It was simply not respectful or acceptable behavior—at all. But I lacked the strength of spirit to confront the issue and establish clear boundaries with them.

It was clear to me that we needed to establish a "new normal" with John and Sally; one of respect of privacy and property that truly was "normal." But I was too afraid of confrontation, possible rejection, and no longer being liked or accepted by our neighbors. It felt like too great a risk for me to take to confront them. I simply had not yet gained the level of courage necessary to confront others, or to set and maintain healthy boundaries with anyone in my life. So I allowed Sally to continue to barge into our home unexpectedly, at will.

As the weeks turned into months and years with Sally popping in unannounced as she pleased, and she and John coming into our yard whenever we were outside, my frustration grew into a cancer of resentment. The issue continually invaded my thoughts like Sally invaded our home. The circumstance that Jeff and I were allowing kept me in a state of anxiety, frustration, and anger. The fear of rejection was so deeply rooted in me, I didn't know how to establish healthy boundaries with anyone. So, I continued to allow our otherwise kind and helpful neighbors to share ownership of our home and property, even though it was costing me (and our family) emotionally.

Inside myself, I was furious over their continual disregard for our family's privacy and common courtesy. I was furious over being taken off-guard at any given moment by Sally's intrusive habit of entering our home at will. As a stay-at-home mom, the constant, unexpected interruptions were harder on me than on Jeff because her sudden appearances occurred more often during the day, while he was at work.

I talked with Jeff on several occasions about my frustration and fury. It didn't seem quite so abnormal or frustrating for him because he'd grown up with Sally entering his childhood home and he didn't experience it nearly as often as I did; however, he was annoyed at her inappropriate behavior. Like me, though, he didn't have the strength of spirit to confront.

We both knew it was our right and responsibility as individuals and adults, and as examples to our children, to speak up about unhealthy and inappropriate behaviors. We needed to speak truthfully with John and Sally to tell them that their lack of respect and courtesy for our family's privacy was unacceptable—regardless of their good intentions or the relationship they had shared with Jeff's parents. We just didn't have the inner courage or the knowledge how to best go about this.

I felt trapped by my own feelings of inferiority to people around me. Even though I wanted to talk to Sally about the issue, my insecurities kept me silent. But the issue kept me on edge—jumpy, irritable, angry, and resentful; and these rancid emotions continually streamed out to my family. They were living with my resentment and anger as a lifestyle, too. We could not enjoy or embrace peace in the privacy of my own home and I was punishing my own family for it, instead of going to the root of the problem.

We needed help.

It's not easy to change our behaviors or set healthy boundaries. How we were shaped by our parents and our environments as children carries over into our adult lives, and our children's lives, from generation to generation, unless we gain the knowledge and courage to change. As we grow in Christ by learning and practicing the principles of His Word, we become more mature and confident to change for our benefit and for the generations to come.

As Jeff and I continued to grow in intimacy with each other and the Lord, God began to reveal to us through His Word that it wasn't His desire for us to live without boundaries. A lack of boundaries prevents security, safety, and the freedom and peace that He desired for us.

The choice to change was ours to make, though, and change is never easy.

We remembered Romans 12:2 (NIV), "Be transformed by the renewing of your mind." This is what Jeff and I needed to do. We needed to renew our minds to align with God's principles which are life-giving, freeing, and peace-bearing.

As we grew in our knowledge of God and His principles for living, we began to understand more clearly and fully our worth in Jesus Christ. We began to grow in courage, strength of character, mind, emotion, and spirit to break away from childhood experiences which had skewed the truth of how God sees us and what He desires for us. We began to see that our past experiences (which had fostered insecurities in us) had been hindering us from enjoying the life of true freedom and peace that Christ desires for every individual and family.

Change within us could and would happen. In the process, we experienced many different emotions: relief, sorrow, anger, anxiety, joy, and peace.

We experienced relief at the realization that we didn't have to live in bondage to people's desires, expectations, and circumstances which were contrary to the needs of our family and the desires God had for us as a family and individually.

We felt sorrow, and even anger, when we realized the years of intimacy, privacy, and freedom we had lost due to our lack of courage to set appropriate boundaries.

We experienced anxiety over the truth that we needed to be "strong and courageous" in establishing and maintaining healthy boundaries, because this would require confrontation.

As scary as change is, though, it's necessary if we desire to live fully in the freedom and peace that God intended for His children.

Finally, we also experienced joy and peace in knowing that our future could be and would be very different. We looked forward to embracing as individuals, as a couple, and as a family, a newfound freedom and peace—a "new normal."

We realized we could create a tangible boundary with our neighbors, shortly after we got our Golden Retriever, Lacey. We wanted to enclose our backyard with a fence to contain and protect our new family pet. We were not yet in a place of mind and spirit to forwardly confront John and Sally, but saw this opportunity to put a fence up as a step in that direction.

Jeff was in our backyard, measuring our property and determining our true property lines. When John and Sally saw that he was busy taking measurements and walking the physical boundary, they came over, inquisitive about what he was up to. He shared that we were planning to put a fence around our property so our new dog could freely and securely roam and play with our girls. John and Sally were opposed to a fence, offering that there had never been any fences between them and Jeff's parents. Wow, how this truth spoke to the generational lack of boundaries between our two families!

Although we had not yet been bold or brave enough to share with them our desire to establish physical and relational boundaries between our families, we had hinted at our desire at various times. So, perhaps part of their opposition was that a physical fence would serve as a visual reminder of those desires.

Seeing Jeff's determination to enclose our backyard, John and Sally suggested that he enclose *both* of our backyards—as *one* large encasement of our properties!

Absurd!

Their suggestion revealed to Jeff and me just how deeply rooted the lack of boundaries had grown through the years—to commonplace and acceptable. We realized to a greater extent how necessary it was for us to be courageous to establish a "new normal" with our neighbors.

We began by installing the physical fence around our yard.

Once the fence was up, I was excited because I felt it would, in fact, not only be a safety boundary for our dog and our girls, but also a tangible reminder to our neighbors that we desired relational boundaries as well. I was hopeful that our new fence would discourage John and Sally from coming into our backyard so freely at will. Also, the fence would allow our family the freedom to enjoy playing and growing together with privacy, in our own backyard.

The very next morning, as I was looking outside my kitchen window into our backyard, I was shocked and dismayed to see John and Sally carrying their lawn chairs inside our fence, then build a fire in our fire pit where they began to burn their trash! They sat down in their chairs to read their newspaper while it burned, as if it was their own fenced-in back yard! Amazing! I was truly stunned! I couldn't believe my eyes!

In those moments, I realized how truly out of balance and unhealthy our neighbors' relationship with Jeff's parents had grown through the past generation into ours. We desperately needed to take action, with strength and courage, to speak truth to them.

Jeff was home at the time and I called out to him to look out the window. He was as stunned as I was. We could hardly believe our eyes!

I asked him, "What do you think this means?"

His reply confirmed what I already knew in my heart we needed to do. "I think John and Sally are trying to tell us that our visible boundary is not really a boundary at all between our families."

This was truly a sobering moment for us as we realized just how out of hand and truly ridiculous the issue had grown. I had known, deep inside for all those years, that our neighbors' behavior was not normal, lacking common courtesy and respect of privacy. Now my eyes were clearly opened to how wrong, how disrespectful, how inappropriate our circumstance was.

I asked myself: *Who just walks into another person's home without knocking first? Who just makes themselves at home in another person's fenced yard, much less builds a fire and burns their trash, without asking permission??*

I tried to imagine myself doing these things to a neighbor. The thought was completely absurd to me. But there we were, allowing the very circumstance I couldn't even imagine!

Jeff and I purposed to talk to John and Sally. We wanted to do this with genuine love and care, but with clarity to establish and enforce a "new normal."

They were nice people, but nice people can have poor behaviors. Jeff and I had poor behaviors by not establishing and enforcing boundaries as soon as we had moved into our new home. We had poor behaviors by continuing to allow our neighbors' lack of respect for our family and property—and for so long.

We knew that none of this would be easy. We understood that they had lived for many years in an "open invitation" environment with Jeff's parents, which they had all embraced as normal.

We understood that we had allowed the lack of boundaries to continue. So, we knew it would not be easy to confront them on this issue nor set appropriate boundaries and enforce them; but a new normal was necessary for our family.

After much prayer and discussion, Jeff and I agreed that he would go alone to our neighbors' home because he had known them for practically his entire life. With love and care, but also with clarity, he would share with them the boundaries we desired and planned to enforce.

As silly as it may sound, Jeff actually had in hand a printed list of boundaries to give to Sally and John in the hope that the tangible list would serve as an additional visible reminder that we were very serious about creating a new normal.

While Jeff was gone, I replayed our own attitudes and behaviors in my mind and heart. I reasoned that even though we had not openly and honestly confronted either Sally or John prior, we *had* given them subtle hints, numerous times, with the hope that they would begin to practice common respect. It had appeared that they'd understood those subtle messages because they had changed temporarily, for short periods. The change never lasted. The root of "no boundaries" had grown very deep through the years. Changing habits of lifestyle which were so deeply rooted would not be easy, but it was necessary.

Jeff and I knew that we would have to remain steadfast in our decisions for our family. Confronting John and Sally in love, then standing firm in what was right, would prove to be a stretching experience of growth for us all. We were not only asking Sally and John to change, but asking ourselves to change. We knew it was the right thing to do.

Jeff was gone for about 45 minutes and I wondered what could possibly be taking that long. I anxiously awaited his return, wondering how John and Sally had responded to him and to our list.

When he finally returned, I was full of questions, anxious to know all the details of their conversation and the outcome.

Jeff shared with me that after some small talk he had explained with courtesy and respect that their relationship with Jeff's parents had been a different kind of relationship than we desired for our own family. He shared kindly but firmly that while it had been acceptable for his parents and them to openly come and go between their two homes and properties at will, this was not acceptable behavior for our family.

Jeff shared with me that John and Sally had appeared receptive to a new way of interacting as neighbors. We were so relieved, and excited for a fresh, new start.

Naturally, the relationship between the four of us was a little awkward and strained for a time as we all attempted to go about our day-to-day lives, practicing this new normal. Change is always uncomfortable in the beginning because it's new and different. It takes time and determination to root out old habits and grow into new, healthy ones. But with the four of us invested in working at a new normal, over time we all grew into it—with our friendships intact.

I felt a newfound freedom in my home, knowing I could leave my door unlocked and no longer be taken off guard by a sudden disruption to our family's activities. I was experiencing God's Word—alive in my life—from Psalm 16:6: "The lines ["boundary lines" NIV] have fallen to me in pleasant places; indeed, my heritage is beautiful to me."

God had given us the inheritance of a new home for our family, and we had needed to seek out the just and rightful boundary lines, both literally and spiritually. We were finally able to enjoy peace, privacy, and freedom in our home because we had tried and tested God's principles and found them to be true and trustworthy.

I've heard it said that we teach people how to treat us by our own actions, whether good or not so good. I experienced this to be true in our relationship with Sally and John.

God continued to encourage us to set healthy boundaries in all our relationships as well. I had to truly consider how I allowed people to treat me and address me. Was it with consideration, courtesy, and respect?

I realized I had to first learn to see *myself* as God sees me, and learn to treat myself with consideration, courtesy, and respect while mirroring these values to others in the way I treated them. Luke 6:31 says, "Treat others the same way you want them to treat you."

ණ ❧

Just as we had finally established boundaries with our neighbors, the next major adjustment for me would be to address those in my life who were continually issuing callous and hurtful words to me.

Through my childhood and into my adult life, there were those close to me who had tagged me with degrading nicknames and made hurtful references to me and about me. I lived in a continual discomfort of heart and mind because I had allowed these unkind behaviors to continue against me, well into my adult years.

Words spoken to me and about me had been a very sensitive and tender area of issue for me since as early as I could remember, because this was a constant in my life that grew to be a well of hurt and shame. I shared previously that, as a child, some peers had repeatedly called me "goofy," and I grew up believing this lie about myself. And that was followed by years of name-calling and bullying, so it was, indeed, a very sensitive issue. "The tongue has the power of life and death . . ." (Proverbs 18:21 NIV). I knew this to be so true.

Although I had gathered the courage to tell the teacher that classmates were calling me "goofy," speaking up in my own defense had resulted in further belittling and the inexcusable, "We were just joking around." This taught me to remain silent.

For many years as an adult, I didn't stand up for myself to those close in my life who called me belittling names and made demeaning comments to and about me, all under the guise of "teasing." I didn't speak up and share how hurtful this was because I feared their further teasing, and their rejection. I lived miserably inside and out—just as I had with the ongoing intrusion of our neighbors.

I've also heard it said that people won't remember what you said, but will remember how you made them feel. What an impacting statement this was for me because I *did* remember, and carried inside me my every day how name-calling and teasing hurt me so deeply. It hurt just as much as an adult as it had throughout my growing up years.

Teasing and demeaning is hurtful.

Teasing and demeaning devalues.

Teasing and demeaning reaps the belief that one is worthless and helpless.

Teasing and demeaning was not a "joke" to me; it was death of my spirit and in direct conflict with how God's Word says He sees each of us — as His deeply loved and valued creation, His adopted children of great worth; heirs to His kingdom. Teasing and demeaning is in direct conflict with how He specifies through scripture that we are to treat one another. Just one example is: "'Love your neighbor as yourself.' There is no other commandment greater than these" (Mark 12:31).

Continuing to allow others to talk disrespectfully to me and daily carrying that well of hurt and feelings of worthlessness inside me disabled me, bound me, and prevented me from being all God desired me to be as a grown woman of God, a wife, mother, daughter, sister, aunt, friend . . .

Due to my childhood experiences, I had naturally grown to crave *affirming* words—my greatest emotional need. Word of affirmation was my highest "love language," the thing that filled my emotional tank the most. So, whenever foolish jesting and joking was made toward me or about me, I not only felt rejected but also frustrated, angry, wounded, drained, and depleted. Empty.

God's word *repeatedly* tells us to "Encourage one another."* We should use the power of our words to affirm, lift up, build up, and fill up others emotionally so they can fully grow into all God created them to be as unique and valued individuals and to fulfill their destiny in Christ. (*1 Thessalonians 5:11, 4:18; Hebrews 3:13, 25:10 partial list)

There are different kinds of boundaries we can allow people to cross. I had no clear emotional boundaries set for myself. By my own choice and action, this had to be confronted. Name-calling and belittling had to stop.

God gave me several opportunities to practice the principles of His Word regarding offenses by others—those closest to me who I had allowed for too many years to speak hurtfully to me and about me. His instructions for dealing with an offense are found in Matthew 18:15-17:

> If your brother sins, go and show him his fault in private; if he listens to you, you have won your brother. But if he does not listen to you, take one or two more with you, so that by the mouth of two or three witnesses every fact may be confirmed. If he refuses to listen to them, tell it to the church; and if he refuses to listen even to the church, let him be to you as a Gentile and a tax collector.

In the beginning stages of standing up for myself to establish clear and right emotional boundaries it didn't go as well as I'd hoped. Standing up for one's self is not easy, and again

I was met with the same unacceptable excuse I'd heard too often throughout my life: "I was just joking with you; it's no big deal."

To me, it was a *very* big deal.

When family or friends called me teasing names or spoke hurtfully about me, regardless of their intent, it fed the very deep root of rejection that I was striving to root out.

To effect right change, we must be determined, and we must be strong, and courageous to obey God's Word.

I began to stand up for myself more and remain firm with those adults who continued to speak hurtfully to me. Just like the case with our neighbors at first, when I'd speak to those belittling me, it would cease for a time and the relationships were better; but again, old habits and patterns easily resurface. The habit of speaking hurtfully to me, and my pattern of allowing it, continued to leave me feeling just as hurt, frustrated, angry, and drained.

I was beginning to understand more fully that deeply-rooted issues must be dealt with *at the root*—not simply on the surface. Surface attention to unhealthy thinking and behavior habits is simply a temporary fix. Surface attention doesn't enforce real and lasting change.

So I made the decision to dig deeper within myself, to the root of rejection I had lived with for so long, and apply God's repeated instruction and encouragement which would eventually make me free: I needed to be strong, and courageous to establish clear boundary lines which would ". . . fall for me in pleasant places."

With further determination of strength and courage, I shared with my offenders on a deep level: I shared that while their teasing may not be a big deal to them, it was very hurtful to me, and unacceptable. I shared the root of my sensitivity to words—my childhood experiences of being called hurtful names, unkind teasing, and ruthless bullying. I shared how deeply rooted the hurt ran inside me and how the name-calling and teasing had grown into an internal bondage. I shared that I was living my daily life feeling rejected, incapable, without value and worth. And I shared what I most needed from them: affirming words.

I dug deeper still for the strength and courageous to share that their verbal behaviors toward me were not acceptable, regardless of whether they were teasing or not.

It wasn't easy, but I was determined to set very clear, precise boundaries.

Part of loving people as God loves, and His command to love our neighbors as ourselves, is not allowing and enabling people to be unloving toward us.

I had to be even stronger and more courageous to share that there would be needed consequences if the belittling continued toward me, toward my husband, or our children. As painful as it was to state consequences, I knew it was necessary in order to enforce change to lifelong behavior patterns. I shared that for the sake of what is right, and for my wellbeing and that of my family, if the teasing and belittling continued, I would remove myself and my family from the relationship.

Enforcing these consequences would prove to be the hardest.

Like the transition to a "new normal" had been difficult, awkward, and uncomfortable at first with our neighbors, there was a season of discomfort and awkwardness with those I had openly and honestly shared the truth in love but firmness. We worked to grow together into a new normal.

Open communication, speaking "the truth in love," and standing firm in truth is crucial in establishing relational boundaries. What may be fine and acceptable (inoffensive) to one person can be death to another. We each have different life experiences which have molded us; different mental, emotional, and physical triggers that are sensitive; and needs that are essential. It's unfair for us to expect people to know how we're feeling about their behaviors toward us if we're unwilling to be strong and courageous to share the truth in love.

God's formula for resolving hurts and offensives—to live freely, wholly, respectfully, and authentically—is Matthew 18:15-17. Change generally does feel awkward and uncomfortable in the beginning, but the fruit of following God's principles in our relationships results in the "boundary lines falling in pleasant places."

Chapter 6

Turning Your Stumbling Block into Your Stepping-Stone

"He rewards those who earnestly seek Him."
Hebrews 11:6 (NIV)

I struggled with being a forgetful person. This was a true stumbling block in my life.

I would get so frustrated with myself for forgetting things of importance to me, and then be mortified by what people must be thinking about my poor memory! I felt unintelligent and perceived that others viewed me this way. I felt frustrated and unsure why I couldn't remember dates, people's names, and other seemingly insignificant things, yet important for me to remember. I felt self-conscious about my lack of memory and felt that people around me perceived me as a flighty thinker. Later I would learn from my doctor—and God—the root of the problem.

Another stumbling block in my life was poor eating habits. I was addicted to soda and junk food.

I knew what God's Word said about my body: it's a "temple"* of the Holy Spirit and I am to take care of it: eat properly, rest, exercise . . . But in my foolishness and disobedience I told myself, *Well, this is just "my weakness." It's really not a big deal. I do well in the big, important areas of my life; surely eating poorly* *and not obeying God in this one little area won't be that big a deal.* His Word also tells us, "Do not be deceived, God is not mocked; for whatever a man sows, this he will also reap"(Galatians 6:7). (*1 Corinthians 3:16-17)

For years I ate junk food constantly and had sodas every day. These were my "treats" to myself. Junk food and soda was something I looked forward to—even against my husband's pleas for me to cut down on the soda and start eating healthy.

I didn't want to listen. I had pride and didn't want my husband butting in and challenging me to change my diet—even though he was speaking truth. I just didn't *want* to change or listen to those who cared the most for me—my husband and God. Finally, seeing how headstrong I was in wanting my junk food and sodas, Jeff stopped harping on me and put me in the Lord's hands.

God certainly has a way of getting our attention.

When nothing else seems to work, He will allow us to get to the lowest point in our life—even rock bottom—so we'll wake up to the truth!

My poor eating habits were beginning to take me down.

During the day I would have extreme emotional ups and downs and be very moody. I experienced a lot of anxiety and stress on a daily basis and, more often than not, I simply didn't feel good physically or emotionally. These stresses began to get my attention and cause me to become proactive to find some relief.

I spoke with a good friend who recommended that I see her female Christian doctor. My friend was on a prescription drug for similar symptoms, but lifelong issues, and shared that taking medication had made "all the difference in the world" for her.

I could hardly wait to schedule an appointment with her doctor. I was hopeful this would be the quick fix I was looking for. I was convinced. I told myself that I would go to her doctor, get on a prescription drug, and be on my merry way, and everything would be fine. But, soon I would learn that God had a different plan for me, as He often does.

The day arrived for me to meet with my new doctor. I was very optimistic and hopeful upon entering her office.

Just as my friend had assured me, the doctor was, in fact, a warm, caring woman who was very knowledgeable. She actually specialized in treating women who had suffered traumatic pasts. I felt right at home.

She asked me about myself, my history, and what had brought me to see her. I opened up to her and was honest about how I was battling anxiety and stress on a daily basis, and how things seemed to be getting worse. I shared with her that the little things in life really seemed to stress me, yet when the big crises hit, I seemed to be like a rock.

She quietly listened, taking in everything I was telling her, then handed me a written assessment to complete. Examples of varying life situations were listed and I was to rate each one on a scale from 1 to 10, based on how I would respond to each situation—10 being the least favorable and 1 the best. It took me about five minutes to complete it.

After reviewing all my answers, I could definitely see a pattern, although I was still not sure what the assessment was leading to.

After quickly evaluating my answers, the doctor looked at me and told me something that completely took me off guard. "It appears you have adult ADHD—Attention-Deficit/Hyperactivity Disorder."

I was taken aback by this news.

ADHD!

As I sat there trying to take in this news, my thoughts raced (no pun intended!). Soon, it was as though a light was shining on the many areas of my life that, until then, had simply not made sense to me: how I was so often forgetful, had difficulty focusing, and could not seem to sit still. I was always feeling as if I were being driven by a motor. I felt compelled to clean the house all the time, straighten up things, and buzz around the house, always doing *something*. It was very hard for me to just sit still.

As I listened to her diagnosis, the anxious behaviors in my life began to make more sense for the first time. She had taken all the areas of distress I had shared with her and placed them into one tidy box and given it a medical label: adult ADHD.

I felt sad that I had lived so many years of my life not understanding my behaviors and challenges. Yet, I also felt some relief because she had given me a medical reason for the struggles I experienced on a daily basis. She understood and validated the reality of my issues.

She said she wanted to prescribe an ADHD medication for me to try, and gave me a prescription.

As I drove toward the pharmacy, I let the tears of thankfulness fall freely because I had prayed for answers, and that's what I had gotten—though not exactly the answers I had expected. I thanked God for His goodness in leading me to my friend's doctor and for giving her—and me—the wisdom and insight that I had so desperately been searching and praying for.

"For if you cry for discernment,
lift your voice for understanding;
if you seek her as silver and search
for her as for hidden treasures;
then you will discern the fear of the Lord
and discover the knowledge of God."
Proverbs 2:3-5

God is so faithful. When we seek after Him with our whole heart, we will find Him—and the answers to whatever issues we're facing.

I couldn't get to the pharmacy fast enough.

I wanted to begin the medication that day, certain it would be the quick fix for all my problems the doctor had easily scooped up into a single medical term: ADHD. Now I would be able to focus better, remember things better, and have more energy . . .

It would be great, I assured myself.

Well, taking the medication did not take me in the direction I'd hoped or anticipated. Within a couple of hours of taking the first dose, I began to experience several side effects. I tried to brush my worries aside. *This is normal*, I told myself with confidence I didn't really feel. *Just give it some time. You can't expect drugs to work overnight.*

Days passed with the side effects going from bad to worse—increasing instead of decreasing as I had hoped. I was so frustrated. I just couldn't understand why this was happening!

Confused and disappointed, I prayed over the dilemma. I was confident that God had led me to my friend's doctor. I had asked Him to give the doctor wisdom, and to prescribe the right medication, and also that it would be the right prescription for me. I had believed He would not only honor some of my requests but *all* of them.

So why are the drugs making me feel worse instead of better?! I asked myself.

I cried out to God again with everything in me. (He could handle it!) I asked Him to show me what He wanted of me, and why I was feeling so much worse after He had clearly led me to my friend's doctor and this diagnosis.

In that moment of desperation, He answered me, but the answer surprised me. Like my ADHD diagnosis, His answer certainly wasn't the one I had expected, *or* wanted to hear. But I knew with everything in me that it was God, my Father, speaking to my heart cries.

"I did indeed lead you to that doctor," I heard Him say in my spirit. "You're right in this, but I led you to her so the root of the problem would be exposed to you, so you could deal with the *root* rather than simply glossing over it, or covering it up with a quick-fix drug."

He affirmed in me that I did, in fact, have ADHD and that until I had seen the doctor I would have continued to carry on undiagnosed, and not deal with the root of the problem. He also revealed that He wanted me to do the hard thing again. Not drugs to cover the symptoms but to treat the *root* problem, and in the way He knew was His best for *me*: the natural route to better health.

Now don't get me wrong; I'm not at all against prescription drugs in any way. My first stop after my doctor's visit was straight to the pharmacy! God can, and does, use medications which are vitally important and life-giving to many. The right prescription can be a wonderful and right source of help.

I had eagerly filled my prescription and took the first dose that very day, and each day after, willing to stay on it although it was clearly adding to my problems. God had simply revealed that—for me—He had a different plan.

He deals with each of us as the unique individuals He created. There are no persons identical in every way. He's intimately aware of all our unique needs, so His plans for me were different from His plans for my friend. Her needs were not a clone of my needs. She was on a prescription drug she truly needed to be on for her specific issues—like a diabetic needs to have insulin. His answers for her had given her a quality of life she had never known before.

That's what I wanted, though: a quality of life I had not known. And I wanted His direction for me to be an easier one than He apparently had in mind.

My first clue that a prescription was not the route he wanted me to take could have humorously been when the pharmacy clerk handed me my prescription. Eager to see what the medication looked like, and eager to take the first dose, I ripped open the package—only to find that I'd been given some man's prescription by mistake: Viagra! Certainly not what I needed! I had to (embarrassingly) share with the clerk that I'd been given the wrong prescription.

My second clue should have been that the prescription the doctor ordered was actually giving me the side effects that the drug warning listed as "rare!"

God spoke to my heart again as I sat in our home office, crying out to him. "Angie, *you* don't *need* to be on medication. You need to get off the sodas and junk food and start eating healthy."

As strange as this is going to sound, as soon as I heard this I felt a strong prompting to go to my laundry room and look inside the cabinet above our washer and dryer. In the moment, I had no idea why I felt inclined to do such a thing, but I followed the prompting. I went to the cabinet and opened the door.

I was shocked by what I found there: a book that, amazingly, I had never seen and didn't even know we had! It was titled *Dealing with ADHD Naturally*. I gasped in amazement as I pulled it out. *I didn't even know we had such a book! Let alone where to find it!*

God had supernaturally led me to a book which was sitting inside my laundry room cabinet, a book I'd never seen in our house or even knew we had; so I knew without a shadow of a doubt that it was the Holy Spirit who had led my steps. Finding that book (and in the laundry room of all places!), by a prompting in my spirit was all the confirmation I needed to assure me that God had, in fact, spoken to me.

As I sat in our laundry room, pouring over the pages of the book, I was amazed how intimately involved God is in *every* detail of our lives! Taking all this in while looking through the book, and knowing He wanted me to take this natural path, part of me wanted to scream *No! No! This is not the Lord speaking to me; it's just a coincidence!* I loved soda and junk food so much! But I knew they had become a crutch for me. I had become dependent on soda and junk food to get me through the day, like an addict depends on a drug to get high. I was so used to and dependent on the sugar high that soda and junk food gave me, it *had* become an addiction. And that addiction—and the gross effects inside my body—needed to be cleaned out.

God is so intimate (and humorous). He very often uses symbolism to drive home His desires for us so we don't lose sight of His direction. He could have placed that book anywhere in my house, yet He'd purposely chosen my laundry room as a symbol that I—not a prescription—needed to "deal with the dirty mess" of junk food and sodas contaminating my body like dirty street drugs and get CLEAN.

I loved the taste of soda and, like a drug, I literally craved it.

When my family would go out for dinner, I wouldn't be satisfied with just one soda. I often had three refills. So, the thought of getting completely off soda sounded like a nightmare at that moment. But as I sat there, just me and God, I could sense He was speaking to me again in His "still small voice" (1 Kings 19:12):

"Angie, do you love Me?"

"Yes, Lord, you know I do."

"Angie, do you trust Me?"

"Yes, Lord, of course I do."

The last and hardest question was, "Angie, will you obey Me in this?"

I hesitated, but only momentarily. "Yes, Lord, I will."

This intimate conversation with my Creator brought to my mind a similar conversation He'd had long ago with Abraham, a great man of faith, when He'd ask him to take a much, much harder path of trust and obedience. The symbolism in this passage to my own encounter with God was striking.

Just as God had spoken to me to go to my laundry room, where my faith and trust in God would be tested, He told Abraham to go to a specific place where his faith and trust in

God would be tested (though far greater). Genesis 22:9, it says ". . . they reached the place God had told him about."

God had told Abraham to sacrifice the most treasured person in his life and heart—his son. And God was only asking me to sacrifice junk food and soda!

Abraham did not try to reason this out with the Lord (though I'm sure it had to have been the single hardest act of obedience in his life to consider). He simply obeyed God in faith and trust, and God *richly blessed him.*

Abraham was completely obedient to all that God asked of him, proving his complete faith and trust in God. Just in the nick of time, having proved his allegiance and faith to God, God intervened on Abraham's behalf. He sent an angel whose voice echoed from heaven, "Abraham! Abraham!" I'm sure Abraham was in such a focused state of grief, yet determination to obey God at all cost, that the angel had to shout his name to get his attention!

"'Do not lay a hand on the boy, Do not do anything to him." And God spoke through the angel, "Now, I know that you fear God, because you have not withheld from me your son, your only son'" (Genesis 22:9-17 NIV).

Wow, what a test of faith and obedience!

After I said yes to God (in my laundry room, "the place God had told me about"), I felt an inner peace, knowing I had surrendered my will to His. The thought of making different choices with my eating habits was still hard for me though. I liked my junk food, and I was very accustomed to doing things *my* way. But as I pondered where "my way" had poorly led me this far, I realized that God's way would certainly be better for me—just not as easy. It would be a daily, sometimes hourly, choice to become transformed by the renewing of my mind.

The next day I didn't have a single soda! I started eating healthy. I knew this was not a time to go back to old habits but dive right into doing what I knew was the right thing for me, in obedience to God's best for me.

I began eating healthier foods and eliminating most sugar. Within the second day, I felt a physical and emotional change. I actually felt good! I wasn't as tired; I didn't have all the up-and-down mood swings I was accustomed to; I felt so much more stable . . . I felt like a new person. I was amazed!

Soda had been my favorite drink and just about the only thing I would drink. About three days into my choice to give it up, I was doing pretty well—until I met up with temptation!

I was getting ready to babysit my niece, and when my brother-in-law arrived to drop her off he said, "Oh wait; I have something in the car for you!" I thought this was a little odd, out of character for him. *What could he possibly have for me?* I wondered as I watched him run back to his car.

To my utter amazement, he came back up the drive carrying an unopened 24-pack of soda. Not just any soda; my *favorite* soda!

"This was left over from a party we had at my workplace last night," he said, "and I thought you might like to have it."

Ugh! Yes, indeed I would like to have it, however . . .

It's hard to die to our fleshly desires and habits which aren't good for us, but His Word says, "To obey is better than sacrifice" (1 Samuel 15:22). What a powerful truth! Obedience is what He requires of us—for our good. And following Him doesn't come without the testing of our faith and allegiance to Him.

I graciously thanked my brother-in-law, not wanting to offend his thoughtfulness. He wasn't aware of my choice to change my poor habits in obedience to God; he only knew that I loved that particular soda.

After he left, I immediately got a big, black garbage bag, put all the sodas in it, and stashed it in our garage.

I had passed the test.

When Jeff got home that evening, I told him what had happened and he shook his head in amazement with me. We just couldn't believe a free 24-pack of temptation had just waltzed up our driveway and into my hands—much less my favorite brand!

Jeff ended up taking the soda to work where the guys there would appreciate it.

For every temptation, God makes a way of escape for us. (1 Corinthians 10:13) I'm so glad I didn't cave in to the temptation to have a soda which was literally and unexpectedly placed in my hand.

I love the scripture that says, "My grace is sufficient for you, for power is perfected in weakness"(2 Corinthians 12:9).

Several months later, I reached a point where I could have soda from time to time, like when we went out to a restaurant. Rarely would I get more than one, though. The addiction that was once there was now gone! I had been transformed by the renewing of my mind out of my love for God and my desire to be obedient to His best for me.

There were certain other occasions when I'd enjoy a soda—like when we were having pizza—but the driving force, the addiction, was no longer there. What was formerly a stumbling block in my life had become a stepping-stone.

God has proved to me that He's not only involved in the big issues of our lives, but the seemingly small ones as well. After all, He created us, and His Word tells us that even "the very hairs of your head are all numbered" (Luke 12:7 NIV). This speaks of detail!

He is such a good and loving God, always looking out for His children's best interests.

So many times I had resisted the Lord and had not invited Him into the areas of my life where I most needed His help. I believed some of this stemmed from fear (and pride).

Fear of the unknown can be scary if we haven't learned to truly trust God. For example, we might think to ourselves, *what if I trust God with this weakness or struggle and He requires something of me that I feel I cannot give—or, quite honestly that I wouldn't want to give up?*

The Lord had tested Abraham to the greatest extent, and saw his true heart: his whole faith and trust in God. Seeing that Abraham would not withhold *anything* from his Lord—not even his dearest, only son—pleased the heart of God.

He said to Abraham, "Because you . . . have not withheld your son, your only son, I will bless you and make your descendants as numerous as the stars in the sky and as the sand on the seashore."

You see, God is not some unfair, mean, taskmaster who wants to take from us those we love, or take from us the things He gave us to enjoy in life which are not contrary to His Word. He simply wants our *whole* faith and trust in Him, our *complete* obedience to His Word, and a right and *intimate* relationship with Him. He wants nothing in this life to hold us hostage or take us down a path of self-destruction.

In His infinite wisdom and goodness, He has given us *so much* to love and enjoy in life, but He knows that we will never truly be satisfied until we've given our *whole selves* and all that we love to Him, and have a right and whole relationship of intimacy with Him, withholding nothing from Him and putting nothing above Him. He is our true, generously loving, compassionate, giving, and forgiving Father.

He said that He gave His Son that we "may have life, and have it *more abundantly*" (John 10:10 NIV). Not less abundantly, but "more abundantly."

He sees our sins, our addictions, the things and people we place higher than Him, and the generational behaviors . . . All the things in our life which hinder "abundant life" and our relationship with Him, and the purposes for which He created us. Because He loves us so deeply and desires us to know His complete fullness—abundant life—He will "prune" areas of our lives that are not spiritually, emotionally, mentally, or physically healthy for us; areas that we're clinging to more tightly than we're clinging to Him.

He is our Creator and Holy Father, and He wants to be *first* in our lives above all people and *all* things. Just as He responded so favorably to Abraham's complete obedience and faithfulness, He wants to demonstrate to us that He "is able to do far more abundantly beyond all that we ask or think, according to the power that works within us" (Ephesians 3:20).

Chapter 7

Embracing God's Plan and Surrendering Yours to Him: A Purpose in the Pain

"Those who sow with tears will reap with songs of joy."
Psalm 126:5 (NIV)

Our family arrived at church one Sunday morning to learn that our pastor was ill. A guest pastor would be speaking instead. We had heard the guest speaker several times in the past and revered him as a Godly man, gifted in the prophetic; so I was very excited, yet apprehensive, about hearing him that morning.

Jeff and I were going through a dry and difficult time, so I was hopeful, believing that God would use the guest pastor to speak an encouraging word to us specifically about our circumstances which would help us move forward with renewed hope. I didn't realize until later how I was putting my hope and trust in a man rather than in my Father, God. I was so desperate to hear *something* encouraging about our circumstances that I was, in a sense, putting the visiting pastor on a pedestal.

As it turned out, Jeff had overlooked that he was scheduled to teach the children during the worship service that morning, and wouldn't be in the service with me as I had anticipated.

I felt resentful that he would miss the service, and frustrated because I had convinced myself that God would have a special word for *both* of us that day. The morning was not going according to my desires.

Looking back, my reaction to the overlooked teaching schedule should have been my first clue that my attitude was not right. I had not chosen to trust God and be at peace that He was, indeed, in control of the circumstances and at work in my life and Jeff's. Instead, I had allowed myself to grow anxious rather than applying and obeying Philippians 4:6, "Be anxious for nothing, but in everything by prayer and supplication with thanksgiving let your requests be made known to God." I had not trusted that God had ordered our steps that day and had the best plan in place—which included Jeff working with the children.

In my carnal, limited, human thinking and reasoning, I assumed that because the visiting prophetic pastor was there to speak that Jeff was supposed to be in service with me. The danger of human reasoning and assumption is that we can miss God's greater plan. His plans and purposes are much higher than ours, as He states in Isaiah 55:9, "As the heavens are higher than the earth, So are My ways higher than your ways And My thoughts than your thoughts."

Seated in the service alone that morning, I knew God was present; the message from the visiting pastor was timely, relating precisely to what Jeff and I were experiencing at the time. But I was not able to fully receive God's Word because my mind was consumed over Jeff not being in the service with me to hear the message. I had not surrendered my thoughts to the fact that God was truly in control and had placed Jeff exactly where He wanted him that morning: teaching and ministering to the children. I allowed the cares of my life and my own desire to take control of my thoughts and attitude, and to take higher priority over fully receiving the Word of God.

At the close of the service, still hungry for a prophetic word specific to our circumstances, I made my way down to the altar. Again I was disappointed. The word spoken over me at the altar was not specific to our circumstances as I had hoped for. Although the guest pastor's words *were* encouraging, I chose not to receive them as such; my disgruntlement caused me to reject the words.

After the prayer, still hungry and determined for more from God, I rushed to the back of the building where Jeff had been teaching to urge him to go to the sanctuary to receive a word from God through the visiting pastor. When I arrived, he was engaged in conversation with a group of teachers, but because I was so bent toward my own agenda and blinded by my disappointments and the urgency for things to go my way, I was oblivious to the fact that God was critically at work in that conversation.

I rudely interrupted and insisted that Jeff hurry to the sanctuary. I was stubbornly taking on the responsibility of the Holy Spirit which was not mine to bear. I presumed God had a word for Jeff, when indeed the Holy Spirit was at work with Jeff right there among the children's teachers.

Out of love and respect for me, and not wanting to embarrass me in front of the group, Jeff cut his conversation short and followed me back to the sanctuary. To my further disappointment and aggravation, we found a long line of people waiting to receive prayer. It didn't appear that Jeff would have an opportunity after all, so he hung back rather than taking a place in line.

I was still so convinced that God had a word for Jeff that I grew further frustrated that Jeff was not being more proactive to join the line. Instead, he seemed to be completely at peace just standing there, assessing whether or not he should join the line.

A man from our congregation approached him and engaged him in conversation, sharing encouragement with Jeff.

As it turned out, by God's design, it was exactly the encouragement Jeff needed that day.

What I gained that morning was a humble reminder of the supremacy* of God:

1) Even when we interfere with His plans, they cannot be thwarted; He works for our good.

2) He is truly intimate and powerful in our lives—despite our human tendency and efforts to have our own way.

3) When we're bent toward having our own way, we're often blinded to the important work God is doing right before our eyes.

(*Job 42:2; Isaiah 46:11; Daniel 4:35; Romans 8:28; 1 Corinthians 2:9; Ephesians 1:11; 1 Timothy 6:15 partial list)

I knew how important it was to follow the leading of the Holy Spirit instead of my own agenda, but sadly I had not put this into practice that morning. Consequently, I missed the fullness of God's blessing and peace in my own heart.

I had put my faith in a man instead of in God.

It's so easy in our human mindset to believe that only a pastor or someone else we view as spiritually elite can be used by God when, in fact, God often uses ordinary people who simply trust Him in circumstances and follow His lead. My own lack of trust and sensitivity to the work of the Holy Spirit brought to my mind 1 Corinthians 1:27-29, "But God has chosen the foolish things of the world to shame the wise, and God has chosen the weak things of the world to shame the things which are strong, and the base things of the world and the despised God has chosen, the things that are not, so that He may nullify the things that are, so that no man may boast before God."

I was reminded that we are simply God's vessels, His children in whom He will speak as He chooses in order to accomplish His purposes. He doesn't need our direction, just our willingness and obedience to follow His lead, putting our own self-centered agendas aside for all the good things He wants to display before us and pour into us.

Jeff *had* received an encouraging word that morning! It just hadn't come from the source I thought it would come from, and which I had pushed for. I was reminded that God's thoughts and ways are higher than mine, and always for our best—not second best, *the best*!

Jeremiah 29:11 always reminds me how much God loves me and desires my trust in Him:

> *"'For I know the plans that I have for you,' declares the Lord, 'plans for welfare and not for calamity to give you a future and a hope.'"*

I had been so consumed with my own agenda that morning I had not even thought about asking Jeff how his teaching had gone until later that day. He shared with me that of all the times he had taught, that morning was one of his best experiences! He had walked into the classroom with no human agenda, just a willingness to follow God's lead, and God had supplied all that Jeff needed—both during the service and after.

As further affirmation, Jeff said that an adult helper in the classroom had shared with him after class how blessed he was by Jeff's teaching that morning.

God not only judges our deeds and actions*, He looks at and judges our *hearts*, our motives*. He blesses us when we're willing to follow His lead and be obedient to the direction He has for us at any given moment. It's often not about how prepared we are outwardly, but how prepared we are in our minds and hearts—the condition of our attitudes and hearts at every moment to be ready to receive whatever He has for us: His best. (*Ecclesiastes 12:14; Hebrews 4:12)

God had more than supplied, above and beyond, what Jeff needed that day, and others were blessed as well.

God allowed me to go through that painful process to reveal to me that even though my intentions were good (wanting Jeff to receive a word from Him), they were from a heart of self-serving, control, and demand, rather than from a quiet sensitivity and awareness of God's leading. My own agenda and aggravated attitudes had resulted in me missing God's full blessing and peace for me.

In His loving kindness to me, He gently showed me the true state of my heart and mindset, so that in the future I would recall this painful lesson and remember that His way is always the best way. He has a distinctive plan for me—and for you—in every circumstance which, through our willingness to trust Him and follow Him, will result in His very best, not only for us but for those around us.

There *is* purpose in the pain.

Pain is not exclusive to relationships or circumstances. There were times when I'd become depressed for no reason I could pinpoint—feeling the heavy weight of life in general bearing down on me. I would often try to ignore it, push it away, rather than pray through it to gain from God the good He wanted to bring out of my travailing.

Merriam - Webster defines travail as: "work especially of a painful or laborious nature." Travailing is agony that God can always use for our *good* and create into something *beautiful*, when we have the mindset to partner with Him in all things. Often, though, we don't even know what to pray when we're in pain, and that's okay; we have the assurance of an intercessor to God's ears: Christ, who knows precisely what to pray on our behalf. He says, "The Spirit also helps our weakness; for we do not know how to pray as we should, but the Spirit Himself intercedes for us with groanings too deep for words" (Romans 8:26). Then He goes on to say that our pain is not in vain; there is a purpose for our pain: to bring about a greater good in us and others. Remember Romans 8:28? "God causes all things to work together for good to those who love God, to those who are called according to His purpose."

Children of God—we who have received Christ as our Savior—are
empowered by His Holy Spirit
to mature in our thinking; to no longer resent
or try to escape the pain this life brings,
but instead, by God's grace, embrace
the pain for the good He will bring.
We can grow in the assurance that
He can take what the enemy of
our souls meant to destroy, and turn it around for our best—
a purpose in the pain.

My prayer life through past trials had often sounded like this: *Please Lord, let's get this over with as quickly as possible! This is killing me!* My mind would be so focused on the discomfort and inconvenience of my circumstances that I would rarely pause to consciously contemplate how God was at work in my suffering, what He had for me spiritually, mentally, and emotionally that I might gain through the pain. I've learned over time that God ALWAYS has something amazing which He molds from my mire when I'm willing to be pliable clay in His hands — the Potter's hands.

"O Lord, You are our Father, We are the clay,
and You our potter;
And all of us are the work of Your hand."
Isaiah 64:8

Just as the athlete's muscles are not developed while sitting on the couch watching TV, but rather during the most intensive, strenuous workouts, so it is with our mental, emotional, and spiritual beings. Our spiritual muscles are not developed when we're simply coasting through life, living in mediocrity, not really pursuing God and His divine (and amazing) purpose for our lives.

Our character and strength is developed when we're "working out" with God, wrestling and reasoning with Him in the most intensive, strenuous circumstances. Too often though, we don't seek Him until we're in mental, emotional, spiritual, or physical anguish. Instead of "working out" with Him daily—in relationship with Him through the good times and the bad—too often we wait until we're in a place of desperation.

It's what we do in our day-to-day "workout" with God that will determine our true strength and durability in the worst of circumstances and prove how deeply rooted we are in Christ and His Word instead of in ourselves, our pasts, and our human nature.

Choosing how we will walk out our life day-to-day is really quite black and white. We're either going to choose to do life *with* God or *without* Him. There is no standing still, no middle ground. It's to our benefit to pursue God and His plans and purposes which He established for each of us uniquely, from before we were even conceived and before the seeds of human sin and rejection were planted. It's to our benefit to be in intimate relationship with Him at *all times*—in every circumstance, good and bad, common and uncommon, high and low, joy and sorrow, rest and readiness.

"As the heavens are higher than the earth, So are My ways higher than your ways and My thoughts than your thoughts."
Isaiah 55:9

I'm learning that when I'm "Kingdom minded"—seeking after my Father's heart and desiring to serve Him in His way—all the other things in my life begin to fall into place and come to order.

A minister once said to me, "Your pain is going to pay." *What does that mean?* I wondered. Then I suddenly realized that everything I had gone through in my life, both good and bad, God could and would use for His glory and my own good—if I allowed Him to take the pain and despair that human life and sin brings; if I allowed Him to take the lead in my life and *choose* to allow myself to rest in Him and trust in Him.

The pain and despair I had experienced early in my marriage, before God brought healing and restoration, was such a shameful thing in my eyes. It's not uncommon for a married couple, at some point or another, to hit a difficult time or dry season in their marriage; but I wanted to give the appearance to people that we "had it all together." I wanted people to look at our family and think we were doing life right, when the exact opposite was true.

Jeff and I were both a mess when we were not allowing God into the closed-off places of our hearts where His healing and restoration were so deeply needed.

I was consumed with what people thought of me and my family, and their opinions of us. I was blinded to the fact that if I shared with individuals and couples some of my hurts and struggles, and how God was bringing healing, it might possibly bring hope and healing to them and their families.

The enemy, Satan, wants to keep us bound in our pain and focused on ourselves rather than on truth and authenticity. But God says, "The truth will make you free" (John 8:32).

Matthew 10:39 tells us that when we lose our life for His sake—give ourselves, our daily lives and our struggles to Christ and walk in obedience to His Word—we find true life. We begin to gain the "fruit of the Spirit," which is "love, joy, peace, forbearance, kindness, goodness, faithfulness, gentleness and self-control" (Galatians 5:22-23 NIV).

Losing our lives to Christ means reaching the place in our hearts and minds where we truly care more about pleasing God than ourselves and others. For me, it also meant no longer being consumed by what others might be negatively thinking about me. It also meant a complete surrendering to Him by letting go of my efforts to control life and circumstances—much of which was truly out of my control anyway—and no longer giving in to the pressure of feeling that I had to preform and constantly please everyone. It ultimately meant surrendering my plan for my life to God's perfect and freeing plans for my daily life and my life in whole.

A prime example is how this book came to be.

I had never had a desire to write a book.

I didn't have a college education and I had a real struggle with spelling . . .

I was one of the least likely people to *ever* write a book, and certainly had never considered such a thing.

As the Word of God shows us again and again, God often chooses the "unqualified"—those who are simply willing to be obedient to His direction—to enable us and others to see Him, His majesty, His supernatural power. It's God who qualifies those who put their hope and trust in Him, and step out in courageous faith to do what seems like the impossible.

> *"God has chosen the foolish things of the world to shame the wise, and God has chosen the weak things of the world to shame the things which are strong."*
> 1 Corinthians 1:27

He's proven this truth to me as I've witnessed Him at work so powerfully in my own life—like the *impossibility* for me to write a book! Think about it: if a well-educated, successful individual writes a book, it's really not too surprising. However, when someone least expected does something extraordinary in the name of Christ, the power in that and the credit is shifted to God.

> *God gives His children everything we need to succeed in fulfilling His plans and purposes for our lives.*

God shifted my heart and focus to Him and to the ministry of His Word by removing from within me, over time, the root of rejection and all the ugliness it carried: the self-consciousness; the lies of worthlessness and shame; the lies of inability and inadequacy . . . Even while working with Him to change my focus from myself to Him and His transforming power, I still found that my mind would stray back to 'me' and those lies from the enemy (Satan) I had believed and carried for so long.

There was a time when I thought that serving in ministry would always be glorious. It's not.

In the testing times of ministry, sadly, I'd revert back to my old ways of thinking: *What will people think of me as I'm standing before a group, speaking; or sitting across a table ministering one-on-one with a woman? How will I appear to them and how will they judge me? How will the message I share come across?*

Me, me, me . . .

I found I still had much work to do in the area of keeping my eyes and my thoughts on Christ to complete me, instead of on myself and others.

The self-conscious 'me' mindset was actually very selfish. In fact, it was completely distrusting of God and His power to use me in ministry. Each time I'd fall back into that old pattern, He'd convict my heart lovingly, but firmly, and convey my own thoughts back to me: *Angie, ministry is not about you; it's about those you are ministering to for My glory—not yours.*

At the time, that truth-in-conviction was hard for me to digest. I was still allowing myself to be wrapped up in self-consciousness and a cloak of worthlessness instead of His freeing righteousness.

At any given time, in any given circumstance, my self-awareness and need for acceptance could spring that ugly root of rejection in me, consuming my thoughts with what others might be thinking negatively of me, how they might be adversely seeing me and judging me, which might lead them to reject me. Rejection of me in any form, rather than complete acceptance, was the fear I had to continually battle as I grew stronger in knowing and embracing deep within me that my true identity is in Christ.

It was transforming and freeing when God's truths began to take a stronger and deeper root in my mind and heart, choking out that longtime root of rejection.

Transforming truths included accepting the fact that people are *not* always going to like what I have to say; they're not always going to like how I look; they're not always going to encourage me; they're not always going to be kind and respectful—or even like me! Knowing these truths deep within me, and accepting those truths in hand with the greatest truth— my identity is in Christ—FREES me.

When I take captive every thought to make it obedient to Christ, and work at something " . . . with all [my] heart, as working for the Lord, not for men,"* I have the assurance that He holds the account of my deeds and nothing—good or bad—goes unnoticed by Him. (*Colossians 3:23 NIV)

Christ said in Mark 9:41, "For whoever gives you a cup of water to drink because of your name as followers of Christ, truly I say to you, he will not lose his reward."

My confidence and security is in knowing that He knows the true driving force behind what I think and do, even in secret from others. He is the only One who gets to keep a record of my sins and my good deeds—not people.

I learned that ministry is often a thankless, unglamorous task; and that's okay when my mindset is on *Christ* (instead of myself); and my heart remains pure to Him; and the work I do here on this earth, in His name, is storing up for me treasures in heaven. Then I can choose peace in knowing that I'm fulfilling God's specific purpose: making a difference in people's lives — those who might otherwise have no hope because they don't know God and who they can be when rooted in HIM; and those who simply need to be reminded of God's freeing truths. There is no true hope and freedom of heart, mind, spirit, and eternity outside of Jesus Christ.

As Jeff and I pursued living in our identities in Christ and in ministry to others, I would also learn that there would be times when some loved ones close to us would not be as supportive of us emotionally and spiritually, as we'd hoped, in moving forward into all that God had destined for us.

This was a tough one.

I can honestly say, though, that I was at the point in renewing my mind (a new way of thinking about myself in relationship to others) that I no longer wrestled with this as I once had. I was more fully embracing God's distinctive calling on my life, placing God above all others.

There's no other place I'd rather be than in His arms and in the center of His will for me.

When we're embracing God's plan for our lives,
day in and day out, we can experience
His peace, even in the midst of contrary
opinions from others. When we're truly
walking out what God has for us in this life, we will sense the
smile of God and His favor on us.

For many, it's also a *process* to know the plans God has for our lives.

As I diligently sought Him, He began to make His directions, His plans and purposes for me, clearer. I better understood Jeremiah 29:13, "You will seek Me and find Me when you search for Me with all your heart."

Seeking God was a personal choice I had to make with commitment and perseverance. Seeking Him above others and the perishable things of this life meant talking to Him about anything and everything throughout my days and nights. It meant learning and knowing His Word and putting His commands and principles into practice from the inside out—with my relationships and with circumstances which were in my control and out of my control.

I was choosing to hang in there with Him, even in the driest and darkest times, and the pain began to pay off.

I'm so glad I did not let go of my faith, or my heavenly Father, through those most difficult times, because it was through the pain that I was changed. A new strength began to rise up in me that enabled me to begin to move more freely and fully as the woman, the wife, the mother, the daughter, the sister, the friend . . . God created me to be.

There *is* purpose in the pain.

Chapter 8

Growing Pains

Parenting can certainly be grueling at times and, like ministry, often a thankless task: the sleepless nights, the effort, time, resources; the serving; the hours of prayer spent on our knees on behalf of our children which only the Lord sees. Even so, parenting brings some of the biggest blessings we ever experience here on earth. For those with children, parenting can be the most difficult task God has entrusted to us and truly the most awesome, rewarding responsibility He's entrusted to us. To know we're stewarding and investing in the future generation, and that we're molding and forming a *life*, is truly amazing.

Jeff and I began to realize that it's not usually the major decisions we make that characterize us, but the *small* choices—the things we say and do on a daily basis—that form our true character.

For Christmas one year, my youngest daughter, Karissa, had her heart set on an American Girl Doll. (*Ouch* $!) She wanted a doll that would look *just like her*: dark hair and blue eyes.

I'm like a little kid myself when it comes to Christmas. I love the joy and anticipation the season brings. But mostly, it's seeing the sheer joy on my girls' faces when they open that special gift they've been longing for. Such was the case with Karissa when she opened her present on Christmas morning.

As she excitedly tore into the carefully gift-wrapped box, she was ecstatic to see the beautiful American Girl doll inside, which looked just like her. I had even surprised her by having the doll's ears pierced, just like Karissa.

The doll truly did resemble her and Karissa bonded to her doll immediately.

She is a child who loves deeply. Even at a young age she had a mother's instinct. It was so precious to see her carrying her doll everywhere and to hear her whisper to her that she would always take good care of her.

She had named the doll Nicole, Karissa's own middle name.

Not long after Christmas, Karissa proudly dressed both herself and Nicole in their pretty, red, matching flannel nightgowns at bedtime. She had received the matching set as another Christmas gift. As I tucked them both in for the night, it was so sweet to see her and Nicole snuggled up to each other. But I had an ever-so-slight inclination that Karissa shouldn't sleep with the doll. I wasn't sure why I had that feeling. Karissa looked so happy that I ignored the nudging inside me and didn't give it another thought.

Waking the next morning, I found Karissa disappointed to see that Nicole had red marks on her nose, cheeks, hands, and feet. I realized that during the night she had clung so tightly to Nicole that some of the dye from the fabric of her nightgown had bled onto the doll's face and body.

I tried every remedy I could find to clean the doll, but nothing worked. I was a little frustrated that I had not followed through with that nudging in my spirit the night before when tucking them in for the night. Seeing the stains and remembering that feeling inside me, I believed it had been the Holy Spirit prompting me. But because I didn't understand the *reason* behind the prompting at the time, I had ignored it.

Coming to the end of myself trying, unsuccessfully, to remove the stains from Nicole, I discovered there was actually a "doll hospital" especially for the American Girl-type doll. I learned that I could ship a damaged doll to the "hospital" for repair or cleaning. It was my last resort.

I called the doll hospital to inquire about the dye stains, to see if they thought they might be able to remove them. The representative said they wouldn't know until they saw the stains, and she encouraged me to ship the doll to them so they could try. She said there was no guarantee the stains would come out. Because we had just purchased the doll only a few days prior, she also offered that I could send the doll back and they would ship an identical doll as a replacement! I was so relieved and grateful to hear this. The doll had been very expensive to purchase—and just newly purchased—so to my reasoning, a replacement with a 'perfect' doll was the perfect solution. I only hoped Karissa would feel the same.

I told Karissa I needed to speak with her.

As we sat on the couch together, I explained the situation and her options: We could send Nicole to the doll hospital, with a chance that the stains could not be removed; or we could exchange Nicole for a brand new doll that would look identical to Nicole, but without the stains. I reasoned with Karissa that I believed a new doll would be the best choice.

She thought about this for only a moment then blurted out, "Mom, that wouldn't be the same! I don't want a new doll! I want Nicole!"

Oh, that wasn't what I wanted to hear.

I had spent a lot of money on that doll, and—truth be told—I enjoyed how beautiful and flawless Nicole had been. I didn't want Karissa to keep the one with dye stains all over her.

I reasoned with her some more and asked her again if she wanted to have Nicole shipped to the doll hospital so they could try to remove the stains, or get a new doll just like Nicole.

Karissa was having a terrible time deciding what to do (and my patience began to wear a little thin). She was hoping the stains could be removed from Nicole at the "hospital," but she could hardly bear the thought of being separated from Nicole for the estimated week that Nicole would be in the hospital.

Upon coaxing her to make a decision, she made the difficult one to have Nicole sent to the doll hospital instead of getting a new doll. But she was very apprehensive about being separated from Nicole for so long. She loved her doll and was concerned about Nicole making it safely to her destination and back.

I assured Karissa that everything would be fine. I was hoping the hospital could somehow remove the stains so Karissa could have her 'perfectly beautiful' doll back once again.

We carefully packed Nicole for the trip and shipped her to the hospital.

A few days had passed when I received a call from the hospital, informing me that they were unable to remove the stains. I was so disappointed. Not only because of the money I had spent on the doll in the first place (whose beauty was quickly 'ruined'), and because I knew Karissa would be disappointed; but also—in all truth—because I was hoping the doll would be restored to her original beauty.

I can be like a little girl at heart, and I loved pretty and beautiful things. The doll with her bright red-stained nose was certainly *not* as beautiful (in my eyes) as she had been when Karissa had first opened her present on Christmas morning. In my eyes, Nicole was now *flawed.* I liked everything to be pretty, not flawed.

As I contemplated telling Karissa the sad news, I considered, once again, trying to coax her into accepting the company's generous offer to send her a brand new doll. I knew in my heart, however, that my daughter would want to keep "Nicole." A new doll that looked like Nicole would not mean as much as to Karissa because she had truly bonded with Nicole. She loved her, flaws and all—a true mother's heart.

As I sat with Karissa on the couch once again, and did my best to explain to her that Nicole could not be restored—but the company was still willing to send her a brand new doll—she broke down and sobbed. Gut-wrenching sobs.

Finally, my 8-year-old looked up at me with all seriousness and said, "Mom, this is really hard . . . But I've thought about it, and . . . Jesus wouldn't throw *me* away if I had a bruise or mark on *my* face. I'm not going to do that to Nicole! They can keep that new doll; I'll take Nicole back."

Wow! (I almost got goose bumps.)

My little girl was only 8 years old and what profound truth she knew, and shared! "Out of the mouth of babes . . . ," says Matthew 21:16 (KJV).

My daughter was learning and understanding the true meaning of love—and reminding me of truth! She wasn't going to reject something she cared deeply for based on its outer appearance. *What a wonderful mother she was going to make someday*, I marveled to myself.

Surprisingly enough, though, I was still experiencing my own personal battle about the doll's appearance. Of course, I had not bonded to Nicole as Karissa had. To me, "Nicole" was just a doll (one that *had been* pristine). As precious and truthfully profound Karissa's reasoning had been, there was still a selfish part of me that wanted the doll to be replaced so she would look "perfect" again.

To my shame and self-disappointment, I had actually momentarily contemplated accepting the company's offer to replace the doll, then telling Karissa they were able to get Nicole cleaned up after all. I reasoned, *She will never know the difference.*

I was quickly convicted.

I might be able to fool Karissa, but God and I would always know the truth of my deception and lying. *What was I thinking?!* I scolded myself. I could not deceive my daughter or go against God's expectation of righteousness! I was ashamed that I had even momentarily considered such a thing, and relieved and thankful that I would make the right choice and not follow through with sin.

Oftentimes, it's the seemingly small things we battle—the private issues of our hearts which no one other than ourselves and God are aware of—that can prompt further Godly character in us.

I've gone through seasons where God has put His finger on (and convicted me of) an issue that seemed insignificant—like secretly replacing Nicole—but in God's eyes is sin. Sin is sin, no matter how big or small, and no matter how it's packaged.

As Karissa had with Nicole, God looks at our hearts rather than our outer appearance.

"God sees not as man sees, for man looks at the outward appearance,
but the LORD looks at the heart."
1 Samuel 16:7

God goes straight to our hearts. He looks beyond our intentions, our words, our actions, and sees what is truly on the inside: our thoughts and motives.

Are our hearts truly Godly or ungodly in our thoughts and decisions which lead to actions?

We may be able to deceive people, but we can never deceive God. He's aware of our every thought, our every motive, and the driving force behind all that we think, say, and do.

We can be confident in this: if we're truly striving to serve Him and bring Him glory, our good deeds will not go unnoticed by Him. The Bible tells us that if we give even a cup of water to a little one in His name, our reward will be great. (Matthew 10:42)

The more I dwelled on Karissa's stained doll and her maturely profound conclusion, the more I realized how proud I was of her and the depth of love inside her. No matter how "stained" Nicole was, Karissa would still love her and never reject her—just as Jesus would never reject Karissa but would always love her just as she was.

How precious and telling these truths were to me. She was not going to disregard Nicole just because of how she looked. She was going to love unconditionally.

I began to cry.

I realized the Godly character and depth of love that had been displayed to me by my 8-year-old daughter, and how in that moment my child had become my teacher.

". . . A little child shall lead them."
Isaiah 11:6 (KJV)

After I regained my composure, I quickly called the hospital back, thanked them for their generous offer to replace the stained doll, and explained that it didn't matter to my daughter—or to me—that the doll's stains couldn't be removed. I asked them to please send Nicole back as quickly as possible.

I was surprised and grateful when FedEx delivered her to our front porch exactly 24 hours later. I knew, however, that my excitement would not compare to what Karissa would feel when Nicole was back in her arms.

Karissa was downstairs playing when the package arrived, unaware that Nicole was back. I silently brought the package inside, dressed Nicole in her best outfit and brushed her shiny hair. Then I quietly went downstairs to Karissa, hiding Nicole behind my back.

I told Karissa that I needed to talk to her. She looked up at me quizzically. I broke into a smile and presented Nicole to her.

Her eyes lit up, then filled with tears as I told her how proud I was of her heart and her decision, and assured her that she had made the right choice to keep Nicole— just as she was.

As I stood back in the distance, watching my daughter, I saw her cling to her stained doll and whisper, "Nicole, you're back! You're really back! I promise I'll never let you go again."

Wow! I will always remember that day.

Our daughter was realizing the true meaning and value of something precious to her, and that genuine love is not based on outward appearances. She simply loved and valued Nicole for who she was—just as she was.

I humbly realized that amidst all the bumps in the road and the challenges in rearing our children, Jeff and I must have been doing *something* right for our daughter to display such truth and such a beautiful reflection of our Heavenly Father's love. Though I realized we had made many mistakes as parents, and were far from perfect, Karissa had gotten it right! She had chosen to love, no matter what the cost—just as God loved us so much that He paid the greatest price for our salvation and restoration from sin: the sacrifice of His own Son, Jesus Christ.

"But God demonstrates His own love toward us,
in that while we were yet sinners,
Christ died for us."
Romans 5:8

The Father's love for us is not based on how we look on the outside, or how we perform. He simply loves us because we are His children—stains and all.

What a powerful, humbling life lesson I learned from my precious daughter that day.

Interestingly enough, in the months that followed, I was again challenged by my own outward appearance.

I battled insecurities while trying to lose weight (seeing that it wasn't coming off as easily as it had in the past). I was growing older and I struggled with the process of aging. I began to notice minor changes on my face: wrinkles I had not previously known and some slight changes in my complexion. I battled anxious thoughts and insecurities about growing old, feeling as though my worth and identity was ebbing away with the physical years.

In my eyes, I was no longer as physically beautiful on the outside as I had once been when younger. I still battled some fear that I would be rejected because I was no longer able to hold to the same physical image I once had—a common insecurity for many middle-aged and older women.

I had to again conquer the lie that my worth and value is based on my physical appearance. I had to come to terms with the fact that God loved me, stains and all, and His love for me is not rooted in superficial things like my physical appearance. He loves and values me simply because I am *His child.* He would never reject me, and neither should I reject myself. I was learning to love myself as He loves me.

The Lord was rooting out more and more of my feelings of rejection that I had experienced throughout my growing up years and through many of my early adult years. Yes, people I had considered close friends had rejected me from time to time for selfish reasons, but I could rest in, and be confident in, the fact that no matter how I looked or behaved, my Heavenly Father God, and those closest to me who truly loved me, would not reject me.

It was through these painful—yet needed—growing pains of personal trials that God continued to mold me into the woman He desired me to be: rooted and grounded in His unwavering love. Seeing and embracing my true value, identity, and worth—solely in Him—was further freeing me from the root of rejection.

God is the potter, and we are the clay.
As the Master Potter, He truly has our best interests in mind in every circumstance.

When He puts us on the pottery wheel, it can feel as though we're being crushed, and sometimes like we won't survive the trials we're enduring. But the reality is that we, His children, are SAFE in His loving, molding hands. It's through the molding and the fiery trials of life that God shapes and refines us—not destroys us!

He shapes and builds and refines our character through the trials, to produce His shining and polished GOLD in us—the woman, the man, the parent, the individual He desires us to be for His eternal kingdom purpose.

Chapter 9

Breaking Generational Curses

"For I, the Lord your God, am a jealous God,
visiting the iniquity of the
fathers on the children, on the third
and the fourth generations of those who hate
Me, but showing loving kindness to thousands, to
those who love Me
and keep My commandments."
Exodus 20:5-6

Jeff and I had begun to be very proactive with our own behaviors, to look at the *root cause* of our sinful and unhealthy behavior patterns, not just the symptoms the root presented.

Oftentimes, we would find ourselves responding to people and situations by what had been modeled to us growing up, or by what our childhood experiences had negatively taught us. We were learning that we needed to break off generational curses on a daily basis because they were producing poor behaviors in us.

An example is how we parent our girls. We were learning more and more that we needed to seek God's heart and His design for our family instead of relying on what our past, adverse experiences had shown us or taught us as children and young people. We were learning to be transformed by the renewing of our mind.

Change does not come naturally and transition can often be uncomfortable. In fact, as Jeff and I began to put some needed changes into practice in our own lives and in the lives of our children, we often felt like we were walking a hard, untilled path—one that was unfamiliar to us. Our past generations had passed on to Jeff and me *countless* Godly, solid values of truth and virtue, and treasured traditions we cherished. While we were so thankful for these, there were also—naturally—behavioral traits of past generations that we desired to break off.

I loved what our pastor once said: "God wants our ceiling to be the next generation's floor." How awesome is that?! In other words, we wanted our children to go further and do greater things than we ever had, or the generations before us. I believe this is the hope and intention of many parents, including our own.

The truth is, as human beings, we're all born into sin, just as Romans 5:12-13 states: "Therefore, just as through one man sin entered into the world, and death through sin, and so death spread to all men, because all sinned—until the Law sin was in the world, but sin is not imputed when there is no law."

If we've accepted Christ as our Savior, born again, we're still human and therefore still have a natural tendency toward sin and unhealthy behavior patterns which are often passed down from generation to generation, family to family. For example, many adults struggle with an addiction of some sort. If alcohol, for example, there's a good chance their father or mother, or even a grandparent, may have struggled with the same addiction, and possibly even further back through their family line.

While some generational sins are more obvious and easy to recognize—like alcoholism, domestic or physical abuse, pornography . . . —many other generational sins and unhealthy behavioral patterns are not so easily seen, but are just as damaging and in need of change. Some examples include shaming, controlling, manipulating, intimidating, uncontrolled anger, pride, etc.

The point is that *every* individual and family alive carries a sin nature that trickles down and sometimes floods into the next generation. Both sinful and unhealthy behaviors—subtle or not—cause wedges in family relationships and breakdowns in communication, and more.

The well-trodden, familiar path of past generations is far easier to follow, though. It requires little effort with little-to-no change on our part as parents, caregivers, extended family members . . .

When Jeff and I decided to walk some new and different paths of behavior and establish some new traditions for future generations, it naturally felt like an unfamiliar—and lonely—road. Nevertheless, while not forsaking the Godly path instilled by our parents, there were some new, unfamiliar paths that Jeff and I felt God was calling us to walk, and to lead our girls down. He was indeed becoming ". . . a lamp to [our] feet And a light to [our] path" (Psalm 119:105).

As we grew closer to the Lord and began to seek Him wholeheartedly, Jeff and I made some needed behavior changes. And as we grew closer as a family unit, we also began to establish some of our own traditions, new to us, believing this was God's design for our family. We began to sense more of our heavenly Father's heart, not only for our girls but for our family as a whole.

> *"He will restore the hearts of the fathers*
> *to their children and the hearts of the children*
> *to their fathers, so that I will not come*
> *and smite the land with a curse."*
> Malachi 4:6

We began to realize that a key part of embracing God's plan for our lives was to selflessly pour Him and His truths into our three girls, which meant putting many of our own desires aside for a time—like working more hours to have extra income; personal hobbies which were time-consuming;

taking trips which were just for Jeff and I . . . While these self-desires were not wrong—at all—we sensed there was a greater purpose at that particular time in our lives which the Lord was shifting our focus to. Ministry, for us, needed to start at home.

This singular focus meant saying no to additional activities at times—though good activities. We wanted to keep our focus on God's present purpose: investing in our girls rather than becoming burnt out by having too much on our plates. It was as though God was beginning to reveal and transplant His heart into the two of us. Interestingly enough, the more we poured into our children, the more God continued to supply our needs and pour into us.

One of the deeply impacting sins I had struggled with as a teen and young adult, which I strongly wanted to avoid as a generational curse for my daughters, was sexual sin. I know, for myself personally, the reason why I sought sexual attention: to try to fill the void inside my heart which I had previously not allowed God to fill.

This is the case for many young people who didn't receive from their parents the love, appropriate attention, and time needed for emotional and spiritual growth and wholeness.

While I was the one personally responsible for the choices I made—sex outside of marriage—I also understood that the strong desire in my heart for things that might fill the void were due to emotional needs that had not been met in me by my earthly father: quality time, mentoring, and words of affirmation. Because of these unfulfilled emotional needs, I sought inappropriate, unhealthy attention from boys—a tragically common path many girls take without understanding why.

As a teen and young adult, I had not understood my promiscuous behaviors. I didn't understand what was missing inside me that prompted me to feel so incomplete and emotionally needy that I sought ungodly sexual attention.

With three girls of our own, in light of my personal past experiences, Jeff and I began to see how challenging the adolescent years could be. We were determined to do things differently with our girls. We saw how important it was to truly be involved and affirming with our girls in every way as they grew up, building them up to be emotionally whole.

As new and hard as it was for Jeff and I to change our thinking and behavior patterns to be more focused and intentional with our girls' upbringing, with God's grace and help we began to embrace the challenges they were going through as pre-teens and teens, and purposely seek to make sure they would not struggle with the same issues I had.

When our oldest daughter, Courtney, turned 13, Jeff took her on a date and let her pick out a very special ring which he then placed on order for her. Once received, the ring would serve as her "purity ring," symbolizing the covenant we were going to ask her to make: to stay pure for the future husband God had already chosen for her. This covenant of purity would be between her, us, and God.

"A cord of three strands is not quickly broken."
Ecclesiastes 4:12 NIV

While we made the covenant of purity a very positive experience for Courtney, we let her know how special and serious this covenant was, and that the ring would seal our covenant and was not to be taken lightly.

As we waited for the ring to come in, we began to plan a series of 'bat mitzvahs' which would be fun and also teach an important life lesson. We began this covenant of purity tradition with Courtney, as our oldest daughter, and planned to make the same covenant with our other two girls as they each reached the appropriate age.

When Courtney's ring came in, we decided to take the whole family on a "surprise ride." This was another tradition we had started when our girls were younger, and occasionally did together as a family. They loved it! The rides were usually spontaneous. We would have everyone pile into the truck then simply say, "Surprise ride!"

The girls would try to guess where we were going. It may have been out to dinner, out for ice cream, or a ride to the park. Half the fun for them was in not knowing our destination until we arrived. This activity really strengthened our family bond and created good memories for our children and for us. Even as preteens and teens, they were just as excited with our surprise rides as when they were younger.

The arrival of Courtney's ring would prove to be the most memorable surprise ride for all of us.

With her ring snugly and secretively tucked away in Jeff's shirt pocket, we proceeded as a family to drive down to the Illinois River. This surprise ride destination would be the place for Courtney's ceremony, where she would be presented with her ring. She had no idea what was in store.

When we reached our river destination, the girls were still excited but a bit confused. We had not yet eaten lunch and it was past noon, so they assumed we were headed out to eat. The river did not look like it had much to offer in the way of food, and certainly wasn't one of our usual surprise ride destinations.

We walked down the hill, through the trees, to make our way toward the sandy shore of the river. We could smell the stench of dirty, polluted water. I would soon learn that the smell would work to Jeff's advantage in driving home the life lesson he was about to share with Courtney, that our other two girls would also hear.

He had brought with him a clean, unopened bottle of pure water. He had also brought an empty water bottle. He did a demonstration not only for Courtney's benefit, but for all of us. I was amazed and in awe as I watched him give a visual demonstration to Courtney of the importance of keeping herself pure until marriage. I could sense that this idea was inspired by the Lord.

The setting was perfect; just the five of us in the midst of God's creation. Jeff had us remove our shoes and roll up our pant legs. We were going ankle-deep into the warm but stinky and dirty river.

With the waves gently brushing against our ankles and a soft, warm breeze of God's breath blowing through our hair, Jeff filled the empty water bottle with the polluted river water. Then he held up the two water bottles for Courtney and us to see—a sealed bottle of pure, clean water and a bottle of contaminated, dirty water.

He told Courtney she had to drink from one of the bottles and to choose which bottle she wanted. Of course, without hesitation, she chose the clean, unopened water, and drank from it. He asked her do describe it to him. She said it tasted good and refreshing. He then told her that the sealed and fresh bottle of water represented God's best for her, and that's how sex is within the boundaries of marriage: refreshing, good, pure, unpolluted.

Then he had her take a good look at the dirty bottle and asked her to describe, as best as she could, what she thought that water would be like to drink. She thought for a moment then said it would be the opposite of the clean bottle; it would be dirty, not refreshing.

Jeff proceeded to explain that sex before marriage would leave her feeling empty and let down, just like that polluted bottle of water. It simply was not God's *best*, at all. It would leave her feeling thirsty and unsatisfied, just as sex outside of marriage does.

He explained that in the aftermath of giving her purity outside of marriage, she would be left with the baggage of experiencing something that was not meant to be—as she had described the dirty bottle of water as "opposite" of God's best.

Jeff had her drink more of the clean water and talked about the biblical importance of staying pure for marriage. He then presented her with her purity ring, and she made a covenant with us and God to remain pure for her marriage day.

It was a beautiful experience which I believe impacted her greatly and will always be remembered. We concluded the ceremony by going to one of our favorite Mexican restaurants for lunch. It was a treasured, memorial family time.

Several months earlier (in what I believed was preparation for Courtney's bat mitzvah), God had impressed on my heart to take Courtney on a date. The purpose was for me to share with her some of the painful experiences I had had as a child and as a teen and how those experiences and many of my own poor choices had adversely shaped me and steered me down a highly destructive and agonizing road. I would share with her about the name-calling and bullying I had experienced as a child, the terrifying beating at the park as a teenager; and my choice to give my purity away to Ben, instead of waiting for marriage to the man God had already chosen to be my husband.

I truly sensed it was the Lord urging me to share my experiences with my teenage daughter, but I was having mixed emotions about being so open with her about my past experiences. In ministry, I had shared my testimony with a group of girls in our church youth group; with women gathered at a retreat; and with individual women and teenage girls, one-on-one . . . But somehow, with my own daughter, I was experiencing an inner turmoil I had not known when sharing my testimony with others.

Fear tried to crop up in me, with thoughts that my daughter would never view me the same, but rather as a failure or a hypocrite. The evil one wanted nothing more than to revive the root of rejection in me that I daily worked with Christ to destroy.

I had to make a choice in that very moment that I was going to be courageous over my fear to change the tide for the next generation—my daughters. By sharing with them, I was going to do something new, hard, and unfamiliar in the hope that they would choose a different path, a Godly path. I was purposed to be real, open, and vulnerable with Courtney (and my other two girls at an age-appropriate time) about important life-decisions and consequences which no one had talked with me about during adolescence.

I was determined to break off a generational curse and trust God that the stumbling blocks of my past pain and failures would be stepping-stones to steer my girls in a Godly direction.

Jeff and I desired to see our daughters make Godly choices which would honor Him and spare them all the baggage and suffering I had experienced and had unfortunately carried into our marriage.

My evening with Courtney began with Jeff taking some pictures of the two of us. I desired our mother-daughter evening to be a special, memorable one for Courtney and me. She and I had dinner at a nice restaurant and enjoyed light conversation, having a good time.

Earlier in the day, without Courtney's knowledge, I had packed two lawn chairs and a blanket in the trunk of our car so we could go to the park after dinner, where I would share some of my experiences with her.

After dinner, I commented on the beautiful weather and told her that I would like to take her to the park to share some important things that were on my heart. She seemed a bit curious but readily agreed. I explained that by sharing with her some of the painful experiences I had gone through as a teen, and the ill effects of my choices, my desire was that she would make choices to keep herself pure and wait on God's best for her: the man He had already chosen for her to marry.

As we sat in the park on our lawn chairs, just the two of us, I opened my heart and shared in detail the void which had been in my heart when I wasn't much older than her, and how I had suffered greatly because of my poor choices.

She was very attentive as I shared (as best as I could) that ultimately I desired so much more for her, and that as hard as it was for me to share these things with her, I loved her too much not to.

After I had shared for several minutes, I concluded by confessing to her how vulnerable I was feeling, having shared those personal experiences with her; and that I feared she might feel that I had let her down as a role model, and that she might be disappointed in me as her mom.

Her response so touched my heart, as it does to this very day. With all sincerity she looked into my eyes and told me that she would never be disappointed in me; that she was proud to have me for a mom and believed God was going to use me in even greater ways to encourage and help many women and girls who struggle with rejection. Her last comment to me before we headed home was, "Who knows, Mom, God may even take you all over the world to share your story and help people."

The smile on my face matched the smile of my heart as I thought to myself, *out of the mouths of babes.*

I had stepped out in faith to be courageous over my fear to share with Courtney what God had put on my heart, and my 13-year-old daughter had ministered to *me* by showing me unconditional love and grace, and even encouragement toward ministry.

The outcome of that evening combined with our purity covenant and surprise rides, was more than I could have imagined or hoped for as Jeff and I continued to seek God in training our girls to be Godly young women.

The path of parenting was getting brighter and brighter, and not nearly as hard. God was equipping us with everything we needed: wisdom, grace, patience, unconditional love . . . It was our hope and desire that we would not only be breaking off and preventing generational curses for our girls, but that they, in turn, would train up their own children in God's ways and go even further as parents than Jeff and I had.

As our pastor had said, Jeff and I wanted our "ceiling to be the next generation's floor." We wanted our children to go further and do greater things than we ever had, storing up blessings for our bloodline, showing love to thousands of generations. (Exodus 20:6)

Chapter 10

Trusting God as "Abba"

The dictionary defines "Abba" as an Aramaic word for father, "used by Jesus and Paul to address God in a relation of personal intimacy."

It had been hard for me as a child and young adult to picture God in such a personal way. Oftentimes our view of Him can be distorted, as a distant God who is detached and unconcerned about the seemingly small matters, and sometimes even the bigger issues of our lives. I learned what a deception this is. If God knew the number of hairs on our head as Matthew 10:30 states, this speaks of a God of detail and personal intimacy.

I believe our relationships and experiences with our earthly fathers are key in how we view our heavenly Father as "Abba." For example, if your dad was loving, involved, and shared a close, healthy relationship with you, it would quite possibly be easier for you to approach God as your heavenly "Daddy" (Abba) with the cares and concerns of your heart.

On the other hand, sadly, if your experiences with your dad were of a distant relationship, or perhaps even an abusive one, you might consciously or subconsciously view God and a relationship with Him in that distant or abusive light.

If we believe the lie that God is like a distant or abusive earthly dad who will not take care of us or love us, we will lack the confidence to approach Him with the details of our lives that He desires to help us with. If we believe that He truly does not care and is not good, we will struggle with the ability to trust Him as Abba, and will miss the countless and miraculous blessings He has for us.

The Bible tells us that He "rewards those who earnestly seek Him" (Hebrews 11:6 NIV), and to "taste and see that the LORD is good . . ." (Psalm 34:8). In other words, *experience* a relationship with Him so He can prove that He IS good.

Growing up, I did not experience an intimate or personal relationship with my dad. He was a good, hardworking dad, and I *knew* he loved me, but our relationship lacked the intimacy that I so desired. Consequently, for so many years as an adult, I found it hard to truly trust God. I battled the lie that He did not care about the details which weighed so heavily on my heart. I loved the Lord and had a relationship with Him, but I had built walls of protection around my heart because, just as I had desired intimacy with my earthly dad which I never attained, deep down I was fearful of being let down and rejected by my heavenly Father. I kept the walls up so I would not, once again, experience the pain of rejection.

To go to the Lord and open my heart to Him, with the thought that He might not respond to me, was too painful a risk for me to take. So I kept myself at somewhat of a distance from Him. I loved Him and served Him but I had not truly given Him *all* of me.

God, however, in His faithful love and mercy, put me on a journey which would leave me no other choice but to trust Him completely and wholeheartedly; so that I would *know* how intimate He already was in the details of my life and that He would never reject me or leave me. I had to make a decision to deal with and conquer the stubborn root of rejection inside me, and the decision to stop relating to God based on what my personal life experiences had taught me. I had to face my fears and overcome the *lie* that God did not care and that He, too, would reject me. I had to choose to believe the *truth* of His

Word, that He would never leave me or forsake me. (Hebrews 13:5)

Often, it was the very hard trials in my life that drove me to my knees and caused me to go to the Lord and seek Him on a deeper level than I previously had. God works in the crises of our lives to draw us to Him and into a deeper relationship with Him, and He will allow us to come to the end of ourselves so He—and He alone—can prove to us that He is our deliverer and the One who blesses us. For the believer in Christ, God gives this promise:

"In ALL things God works for the GOOD
for those of love Him,
who have been called to His purpose."
Romans 8:28 (NIV; emphasis by author)

Sometimes His blessings come to us in mysterious ways: through the pain and trouble we experience and the hard circumstances of our lives.

At a young age, our middle child, Kassidy, began to have seizures. At about age four she had her first episode. It struck my heart with *terror*. Other than the common cold or sickness, we and our three children had been blessed with great health; so I had never known before what it was like to be in a position facing a crisis of health with my child, so vastly different and serious from anything I'd previously experienced, and one which offered no known cure—just prescription drugs to help prevent the symptoms but not ultimately bring healing.

As a mom, I wanted the best for my child; so it cut me to the core to see Kassidy experience seizures. I felt so helpless, unable to do anything to stop them.

Her first seizure happened on what appeared to be a fairly normal day for her. I was headed out to do some errands, taking her and my newborn daughter, Karissa, with me. I felt particularly frazzled that day as we left the house. I was still adjusting to a new baby and feeling the demands of all that I had to do that day. The most pressing errand was to pick up some photos at the lab for Jeff's part-time photography business, which we ran from our home.

Although seemingly healthy, Kassidy was being particularly moody and disagreeable, which was out of character for her. Looking back, I realized those signs could have been my first clue that something more was 'off' with her. She just didn't seem quite herself; but in my frazzled, hurried pace, it didn't register in my mind that something wasn't quite right with her. I just fleetingly reasoned that she was being a moody 4-year-old who probably needed a nap.

I wanted to make sure I got to the photography lab and back home before Karissa was due for her first feeding, and hopefully lay Kassidy down for a nap as well.

I finally arrived at the lab and went to the back seat of our minivan to unbuckle Karissa's infant carrier. To my surprise, I found Kassidy sound asleep. I was about to wake her but reasoned that she would be even more grumpy than she'd been when leaving the house, and apparently needed the nap. I would be in and out of the lab in less than five minutes since I'd phoned ahead and the owner knew me well. So I quickly checked on Kassidy one last time to make sure she was okay and sound asleep before I headed into the lab. She appeared comfortable and, as far as I could tell, seemed perfectly fine. So I locked the van and quickly headed inside with the baby to pick up our order.

Entering the shop I found it busier with customers than usual. I was feeling a bit apprehensive as several people were in line ahead of me. I thought I might possibly be inside longer than I'd anticipated, so I spoke to Bob, the owner, and quickly explained my situation: Kassidy was asleep in the van and I really needed to grab our photos and get back to her. He said, "No problem," and quickly gathered our orders.

We had more packages than I had expected, and my hands were full carrying Karissa in her infant seat, so Bob offered to carry the photo orders out to the van for me. I had been going to the lab for several years and this was the first time he had offered to walk out with me to carry our packages. I would soon see that this was God's provision for what I was about to encounter.

Thankfully, Kassidy was still sleeping peacefully.

While I was on the other side of the van, distracted with getting Karissa's bulky carrier inside, Bob went to Kassidy's side to put the packages in and saw that she'd thrown up all over herself, but was still asleep. Alarmed, we could see that something was very wrong. In the short 3-4 minutes I had been gone, I would learn later, Kassidy had been experiencing a seizure.

Although I didn't know, at all, what was happening with her in that moment, the reality was that she was still in a full-blown seizure: eyes rolled back and unresponsive to our voices as we urgently called her name, trying to get her to wake up. "Kassidy, Kassidy . . . Wake up!"

Countless emotions hit me all at once like a whirlwind: gripping fear, thinking my daughter could be dying; guilt and shame for leaving her in the van to make things easier for myself; self-blame for what was happening with her . . .

In my shock, fright, and rapid emotions, Bob had to jolt me back to the reality of the moment and the gravity of the situation. "I need you to make a decision," he urged me somberly. "Do you want me to call 911? Should I call Jeff at work?"

I felt like I could hardly think straight; the whole situation seemed so surreal—a nightmare—but I knew I needed to act quickly. I told him to call 911 and then Jeff at work.

Within moments the ambulance arrived, sirens whirling and blaring. As though through a fog, I could see and hear Bob explaining the situation to Jeff over the phone, then telling me that Jeff would meet us at the hospital.

As I rode in the ambulance with my daughter, watching paramedics hover over her, I could hardly believe how my world had come crashing down in a matter of moments, and how—in an instant—life as we knew it could change.

We finally reached the hospital. Kassidy had regained consciousness and it was a tremendous relief that she was in a state of awareness. I was still very scared, though. I didn't yet know what had happened with her in the van, or what might happen next. I didn't know if something serious was wrong with her or if and when another 'episode' like the one we'd just experienced might happen again. On so many different levels it was *terrifying.*

Jeff arrived just shortly after the paramedics had wheeled Kassidy into the hospital. We ran to each other and embraced, weeping in each other's arms. He was also scared, but relieved to see that our little girl appeared to be okay by then. He shared with me that the normal half-hour drive from his workplace to the hospital had been torture for him. He, too, had been battling thoughts of fear and helplessness, not knowing if our daughter would live or die. He also shared with me that he drove faster than he ever had, making the usual half-hour drive in about fifteen minutes.

The hospital staff ran what seemed like dozens of tests. The hours of waiting for test results seemed to drag on and on. Questions were still running through our minds as to what the results would reveal. *What had happened with our daughter?* We both wondered if her life and ours would ever be the same after this. There were so many thoughts and unanswered questions.

It was during the waiting time, with nowhere else to turn, that I began to cry out to God in my heart. *Where are you?!* I silently screamed. *How could you let this happen to my little girl?*

All of a sudden He brought a memory to my mind. It came with such clarity that I knew, without a doubt, God was speaking to my heart in that moment, reassuring me.

About three years prior, I had received a prophetic word (or promise) from our pastor one evening at a church service. As he was ministering to people who had gone forward to the altar for a touch from the Lord, I went forward. The Holy Spirit was evident that evening. The pastor was working very strongly in the prophetic. When he made his way to me, the word from the Lord that he gave to me was confusing. I saw no relevance in it to my circumstances at that time; however, I chose to receive the word and tuck it in my heart, believing God would make it clear when I needed it.

I had completely forgotten that word from years earlier; but as I cried out to God from that hospital where my daughter's future hung in the balance, He brought that prophetic promise back to me. It was as clear and real in my mind as it had been that evening at church: "Do not fear," says the Lord! "I won't let anything happen to your babies. You can trust me!"

Back when I had gotten that assurance from God, my girls were in perfect health. I just couldn't comprehend at that time why God was telling me not to worry and assuring me that nothing would happen to "my babies." However, God is not bound by time. He sees our lives from the beginning to the end, and all the details in-between.

Years before that terrifying day in the hospital, He knew I'd be facing this unknown, frightening situation with Kassidy. In His love and care for me, He was showing Himself as Abba (my daddy) by reassuring my heart in advance that I could trust Him, and that He would not allow anything happen to my daughter.

One word from God can change everything.

That prophetic message I'd received years prior became my life line at the hospital that day, and the hope that I clung to in the days and months which would follow.

Relief began to flood my heart and mind as I meditated on that promise, but I was still feeling overwhelmed, exhausted, and admittedly battling some fear of the unknown. *What would the days to come be like?* But in the midst of it all, God had revealed Himself as Abba to me. He had heard and answered my cry, knowing three years prior that I would need that promise to sustain me—something real and personal to get me through that scary day and the days ahead.

As I shared the prophetic promise with Jeff, he too marveled at the precision of the assurance God had given to me years before. He also began to feel that God would see us through and help navigate us as we faced the unknown.

After hours of waiting, the doctors and neurologist finally called us into a private room where they explained that our daughter had the disease of "epilepsy."

We didn't understand, and the word "disease" felt like another blow to our raw hearts. We were not very familiar with epilepsy. We had not known anyone with this disease and truly didn't understand what it was or what to expect.

We were further stunned to learn there is no known cure, and that the prescribed medication would be to treat the symptoms (seizures) only. It could not bring healing.

Our minds were in a new whirlwind.

From a medical standpoint we'd been given little hope and didn't quite understand how this disease would impact our daughter's quality of life and her future.

The months that followed would certainly carry trying times which would once again stretch our faith and cause us to cling to the Lord and His promise like never before.

We dealt with several different medications for Kassidy. Each resulted in various ill side effects in her. Her doctor adjusted and readjusted medications trying to find her "target dose."

Although the resulting medication seemed to help somewhat, in the beginning, Kassidy would still occasionally have what is called "breakthrough seizures." This is when seizures happen even while the individual is on a preventative medication. Even though Kassidy's breakthrough seizures were minor, they were still scary for us. Each one brought back to my mind that dreadful day at the photography lab and all the emotions attached: fear, dread, anxiety, guilt . . . Yet, through the days and months, God continually brought that prophetic promise to my heart and mind, assuring me He was walking with us through this and that ultimately nothing would happen to Kassidy.

I was learning to cling to Him—to trust Him as "Abba." Proverbs 3:5-6 became my daily bread:

> *"Trust in the Lord with all your heart*
> *and do not lean on your own understanding.*
> *In all your ways acknowledge Him,*
> *and He will make your paths straight."*

I was learning by necessity how to walk out my faith and trust God on a daily, hourly, basis. Through all the ups and downs, fears and doubts, God was teaching me that He was trustworthy and near. He would not reject me; He would help me through times of uncertainty and fear with Kassidy. He was truly my Abba.

Several months passed and Kassidy seemed to be doing fairly well. The fear was beginning to loosen its grip on me, no longer as all-consuming.

I was home with the girls on what seemed to be just another ordinary summer afternoon. My youngest daughter, Karissa, was asleep and my oldest, Courtney, was playing in the basement family room. It was just Kassidy and me in the living room when a seizure struck her. Normally, her medicine would keep the seizures somewhat under control, and within seconds she would come out of it; but the seconds began to turn into minutes with Kassidy still seizing. That familiar fear began to rise up in me.

"Kassidy! KASSIDY!" my voice escalated with my growing panic.

I quickly grabbed the phone, called my neighbor Ann and explained what was happening. She arrived within seconds.

Together we were calling out Kassidy's name, trying to get her to respond, but with no success. Ann suggested she should run across the street to get our neighbor Jake, a paramedic. I readily agreed.

By the time Ann returned with Jake, Kassidy's seizure had progressed to a grand mal. It was another "first" for us. Until that day, Kassidy had only experienced "staring seizures," where she would stare into space and momentarily be "out of it." Grand mal seizures cause the victim to actually lose control of muscle function and start convulsing. Kassidy was flopping around like a fish on our living room floor and gripping fear consumed me. I had never seen anything like that before—certainly not with my daughter's epilepsy.

Jake had come prepared. Because he was a paramedic he had medication on hand which he quickly administered to Kassidy. It stopped the seizures within a few seconds.

I learned later that day that Jake was supposed to have been at a meeting at work during the time of Kassidy's seizure. He told me he had accidentally missed the meeting somehow—a first for him in all his years of working. It was an additional confirmation that God had arranged and ordered Jake's steps that day, so he would be home, and have the medicine and skills needed to help Kassidy in those critical moments. I had no doubts. God was intimate and God was Abba.

He had once again made provision for my daughter and me in one of our darkest hours, just as He had at the photo lab when Bob had uncharacteristically walked out to the van with me, on hand to call 911 and Jeff, just when we needed it. Like God had with Bob, He had arranged for Ann and Jake to be available to help me during Kassidy's first grand mal seizure.

I shuddered as I thought what might have happened if she and Jake had not been available; but I marveled at the fact that they *had been*, and that Jake had had the skills and the exact medicine, readily available, right when Kassidy had needed them. I knew these were no coincidences. Once again, God had taken care of my little girl—and me.

Kassidy was fine the rest of the day; however, I was still reeling in the aftermath of the day's horrifying events. While I was so grateful for Ann's quick response and level-headed thinking, and Jake's quick response and medical attention, and thankful to God that He had ordered their steps to be there and provide help, I also believed that God had the power to instantly heal Kassidy of her epilepsy, completely—no more seizures. So my thankful and grateful heart invited the company of resentment that Kassidy was still experiencing seizures and we were living with the daily unease of her disease.

What I couldn't see at the time was that my faith in God as Abba was growing through this circumstance, which would ultimately prove Romans 8:28 (NIV): "In all things God works for the good of those who love Him, who are called to His purpose."

I was emotionally exhausted that night.

After Jeff and I tucked our girls into bed, as exhausted as I was I simply could not sleep. I tried to relax but needed time to process the day's events alone. And I needed to grieve.

Nighttime can be unsettling on a normal day, but much more on a terrifying one. So I felt especially vulnerable to the "what ifs." *What if Kassidy had a seizure while Jeff and I were sleeping; and we didn't wake up? What if the unthinkable happened and we lost our daughter?* I just could not bear the thought of it.

It was near midnight as I sat on the couch in the quite of our living room. Everyone else in the family was sound asleep, but I was wrestling with some gut-wrenching fears and questions. In my humanness, I vacillated between the assurance I'd gained from the prophetic word God had brought back to my mind and the reality that my daughter had an incurable disease that had manifested itself it such a horrifying way that day.

With my Bible on my lap, I sat alone and cried out to God with everything in me. I almost yelled at Him, with all raw emotion. I felt I just couldn't bear the weight of seeing my daughter go through the seizures any longer. The scary images of Kassidy convulsing on the floor earlier that afternoon were tormenting me.

"God!" I cried out (this time yelling at Him from my heart, not holding back any emotion), "You have *got* to tell me You will never allow this to happen to her again! *Promise me!*" I pleaded. "I beg of you," I continued on.

I felt like I was wrestling with the Lord as Jacob had in Genesis 32:24. I was determined I wasn't going to let go until I had my answer! "How can this be, Lord?" I cried out to Him, sobbing almost uncontrollably. "You promised me You wouldn't let anything happen to my babies!"

I shuddered again as I recalled the frightening scene in the living room earlier that day--the very place I was now sitting. "It's just too much for me to bear, God," I demanded from the Lord one last time. "Tell me You will not let her have any more seizures," I silently yelled to Him. "You've got to promise me."

As I sat there on my couch, whimpering and exhausted from all the emotion of the day, and "wrestling with the Lord," I opened my Bible in desperation. I searched His Word for answers, for assurance, for comfort, and for peace, and was astounded by the words which seemed to leap right off the pages at me—speaking directly to me. The messages were as clear as though God Himself was standing there in my living room, speaking directly to me in an audible voice:

"A man wrestled with him until daybreak . . .
'I have seen God face to face, yet my life has been preserved' . . ."
Genesis 32:24-30

"I sought the LORD, and He answered me,
And delivered me from all my fears."
Psalm 34:4

Just as Jacob had unrelentingly wrestled with God, I had demanded of Him that my daughter not have any more seizures. And those precisely-fitting scriptures were the ones He'd brought before my eyes.

His Word is indeed "alive and active. Sharper than any double-edged sword . . . "(Hebrews 4:12).

I continued to search His Word, starved for answers, but unprepared for what I read next:

"Concerning things to come, do you question me about my children, or give me orders
about the work of my hands? It is I who made the earth
and created mankind on it.
My own hands stretched out the heavens;
I marshaled their starry hosts."
Isaiah 45:11-12 (NIV)

Wow! I was stunned. I knew without a shadow of a doubt that God was speaking to me in that moment through His living Word. (John 1:1-5)

I felt somewhat like Job, who had demandingly questioned God (as I was), and God had responded to Job by asking him, in essence, who he thought he was to so demandingly question His Creator, the One who is above all and knows all.

God said to Job, "Who is this that obscures my plans with words without knowledge? Brace yourself like a man; I will question you, and you shall answer me" (Job 38:2-3).

His living Word broke me and humbled me. I was in awe that the God of the universe had so clearly spoken to me in each scripture I read (and put me in my place), and that I had encountered Him in such a very personal way. He was not some distant, uncaring God. He was not only my Creator but my *Abba*, telling me to trust Him with the work of His hands—Kassidy. ". . . do you question me about my children, or give me orders about the work of my hands?"

As I then sat quietly humbled on my couch, I began to feel His peace sweep over me in a real and tangible way. He was loving and gentle, quick to forgive and full of compassion. My Abba was washing away my fears.

I repented and told my Father I was sorry for making those demands on Him regarding Kassidy. I confessed that He knew better and His plans were higher and greater for Kassidy than I could know. "For as the heavens are higher than the earth, so are My ways higher than your ways and My thoughts than your thoughts" (Isaiah 55:9 NIV).

I also realized that as much as I loved my children and wanted what was best for them, God was their Abba, too, and He had good plans for them. (Jeremiah 29:11)

I continued to marvel at the clarity and precision of what God had spoken to me through those passages. And I continued to weep from my broken place of repentance. In those moments, I committed Kassidy into God's capable, loving hands. Through tears of relief and peace I uttered the words, "I trust you, Abba." I felt a glowing sense of peace in His presence, no longer carrying the burden of Kassidy's health and well-being alone—He was carrying my burdens with me.

Matthew 11:30 was beginning to make more sense to me. Christ said, "My yoke is easy and My burden is light." *But how could this be when life seemed so hard, so burdensome?* I was beginning to understand that I was not carrying the heavy burden of my children's upbringing and well-being alone. While God had indeed entrusted their care and upbringing to Jeff and me, He never intended for us to walk this journey alone. He sent Christ, His son, to share the burdens of life.

When we are born again in Christ, we become "yoked" with Him, but too often we pull away from Him, straining against His help, making life for ourselves more difficult. God's purpose was for us to be in *partnership with Christ* in raising our children, caring for them, and carrying life's burdens. "His yoke is easy and His burden is light" when we choose to be in true partnership relationship with Christ and allow His Father, God, to be our Father—Abba.

Before going to bed I quietly crept into Kassidy's room. She was sleeping so peacefully and soundly. I went to bed with a peace and assurance in my heart that everything would be okay. God would be faithful to "keep that which I had committed to Him" (2 Timothy 1:12 KJV), and would keep me in "perfect peace" as my mind stayed on Him.

"The steadfast of mind You will keep in perfect peace,
because he trusts in You."
Isaiah 26:3

In the months and years to follow, we had some trying times as Kassidy continued to periodically have seizures, but over time there were fewer, and were farther between. Christ continued to walk beside us and prove Himself faithful.

We had been contending for complete healing and restoration for Kassidy, and perhaps that would come.

As I'm finishing the writing of this book, I share thankfully that she has been seizure free for quite some time. We've been able to gradually take her off the medication. She's an honor roll student who is thriving and enjoying life to its fullest.

I thank my God, who is able to do "far more abundantly beyond all that we ask or think according to the power that works within us" (Ephesians 3:20).

Chapter 11

Having a Heart like Hannah

Hannah burned with a desire to conceive a child. She longed for this with everything in her—so much that she was sorrowful and deeply troubled in her spirit. This one desire consumed her, as we read in 1 Samuel 1.

She was taunted by other women because of her inability to conceive, and her husband did not understand her deep state of grief. She had no one to turn to but God.

In her desperation and grief, the Lord looked on her with favor and showed her compassion. He understood her heart's longing as only her Creator could.

Hannah promised the Lord that if He would give her a son, she would dedicate the child back to Him. This was a huge deal for Hannah because a son was what she desired most.

The Lord saw her heart and He honored her request.

True to her promise, Hannah did indeed give her child back to the Lord to serve Him all his days. And God blessed Hannah even more, giving her three more sons and two daughters. (1 Samuel 2:21)

Hannah gave her dream—her child—back to the Lord, and in the end He blessed her beyond what she could ask or think, just as Abraham had.

We really cannot "out give" God. He taught me this very personally.

There was a time in our family's life when things seemed to be coasting along just fine, by my analysis. I was feeling pretty good about most things at the time, and grateful for God's provision.

Our family vehicle was a green Pontiac minivan. It wasn't, by any means, my dream vehicle (I desired an SUV), but it served our needs and I was content with what we had for the time being. It was an average-size van and I was thankful for the extra seating and space it offered our family of five.

One day, totally unexpectedly, our van "bit the dust." When we took it to the repair shop, we learned that the van had a major problem in the engine. It was ultimately going to cost more to fix it than what the van was worth. It was several years old.

Jeff and I were in a dilemma of seemingly impossible choices: 1) we were facing an expensive repair, completely unexpected, which we didn't have enough in savings to cover; or 2) purchasing another vehicle we didn't have the money for. And we had become accustomed to having no car payment.

We were at the end of ourselves because we were definitely a 2-vehicle family and simply didn't know what we were going to do.

Jeff drove his car to and from work every day and I used the van to take the kids to and from school and other errands and activities. So life had quickly become quite difficult for us while our van sat in disrepair at the repair shop; they were waiting on our decision whether or not we were going to have the repair work done.

Our next door neighbors were retired and had three vehicles, so they graciously loaned one to us temporarily. This worked fine for a couple of days, while we grappled with the huge decision: get the van fixed or start searching for a new means of transportation.

After about five days with no clear direction, though, the pressure was starting to mount and things were beginning to feel awkward with our neighbors. We felt they had been more than generous to let us borrow their car for as long as they had, but we knew this could not go on indefinitely. We realized we had to make a decision—soon.

We were feeling the pressure of it all.

Not knowing what else to do, Jeff and I agreed to both independently seek the Lord on what direction we were to take. Possibly either paying a large amount to get the van fixed—knowing it was older and at any given time something else could, and most likely would, go wrong with it—or get a different vehicle, which would add a car payment we really didn't think we could afford.

After praying, I still felt anxious about the whole situation, not really sensing any direction or leading from the Lord. So when Jeff told me that he felt the Lord had spoken to him and given him insight on what we were to do, I was relieved and ecstatic, thinking that our life would finally get back to normal. However, when he very seriously said to me, "You may want to sit down for this," I felt an overwhelming sense of dread, knowing I would most likely not like what I was about to hear!

I was right.

Jeff told me that after much prayer and time in seeking the Lord's direction about our vehicle dilemma, he felt that we were to *give* our van away—to "sow it as seed" to the owner of the auto shop.

What?!

To say the least, I was shocked.

The owner was a little rough around the edges (to put it mildly), but that aside, Jeff and I were often skeptical if he had been fair in his dealing with us—both at that time and in the past when we had taken our vehicles in for repair. So I was even more stunned and in disbelief when Jeff said we should *give* our van to the man. Jeff's thought was that shop owner could repair it to use as a loaner for his customers, or sell it and keep the profit.

My flesh was burning! I was livid at this absurd idea!

This was not, at all, the solution I had expected—or desired to hear after our long period of waiting and borrowing our neighbors' vehicle! Yet, I knew my husband well enough to be fairly certain that this was the direction we were going to be taking, regardless of my opposition.

To Jeff's credit, he's a fair man and normally consulted me on major decisions. Yet, in contrast, somehow I felt that this circumstance was unique, unlike any other we'd previously faced. Boy was I ever right!

Jeff simply asked me to consider it and pray about the decision he'd shared with me, stating again that this was really what he sensed the Lord desired us to do as "seed planting" with the shop owner. He believed that as we were obedient to the Lord and took this step of faith, God would honor that and take care of our needs better than we could provide for ourselves.

My mind was racing.

Logically, I reasoned, *giving our van away is ridiculous!*

On and on my thoughts flared, and the more I reasoned and tried to figure things out on my own, the angrier I became. I just couldn't justify this decision in my human thinking. *Give our van away? Not only that, but give it to a man who had treated us very gruffly and possibly had not even been 100 percent fair with us? Why should we do that?! This guy didn't deserve such grace, in my opinion.*

I continued to rage in thought as if I were speaking directly to the shop owner. *I'll take my van elsewhere and get a SECOND opinion, thank you very much!* And then to myself, *Why on earth should I give it to him and let him keep the profit?*

The more I allowed my thoughts to cycle, the more steamed I became. Finally I realized this mindset was getting me nowhere. I was certainly out of peace (and patience) and growing more and more agitated by the minute. I was getting nowhere except increasingly upset and frustrated.

Like Hannah, I had come to the end of myself and cried out to the Lord in my distress. As much as it went against my will and emotions, I finally surrendered to Him and told Him I would be in agreement with Jeff and we would sow our van to the shop owner with the belief that God would take care of our needs.

Then my mind took on a different cycle: one moment I was confident in our decision and in the next moment fear and doubt gripped my heart and mind as insecurities rose to the surface. *What are we going to do without a second vehicle? How are we going to get our girls to school? We can't borrow the neighbors' car forever,* I reasoned, *and we can't even afford a car payment to get a new one!* And I'd waver in my commitment to God and think, *This is a stupid decision!*

On and on the thoughts bombarded my mind; and I'd tell myself once again that I had to make a final decision.

Like Hannah, I cried out to the Lord (again) to help me with my fear and unbelief, and resolved to leave the outcome in His hands.

Apart from Kassidy's seizures, this was one of the hardest things I'd ever done in my spiritual life as the circumstances seemed truly impossible any way that I looked at it. But let me tell you, God is faithful, and we truly cannot "out give" Him in our giving to others.

We did as Jeff felt inclined—and more. Not only did we give our van to the shop owner but Jeff had shared with me that he also felt led to go above and beyond: to also give the man what little cash we had in the bank to get the van titled!! But that still wasn't the extent of our giving. There was more: Jeff also felt we should bless the shop owner and his employees by taking lunch to them all as well!

I was even more astounded and amazed.

I had just made peace (somewhat) with giving our van away, reasoning that there was not much we could do about paying for the repair. But this new news—that Jeff was going to waltz right into that shop, hand our van over, *and* what little savings we had acquired for the title, *and* take Kentucky Fried

Chicken to him and his employees?! The whole scenario was nearly too much for me to handle.

In my selfish nature I thought to myself, *why would you take lunch to the guy, too? He doesn't need it. Why don't you go pick up lunch and bring it home to me?!* That sounded much more appealing to me at the moment. But again, God's ways are not our own (certainly not mine), and He will often turn our thinking around—if not upside down in the process.

"Love is patient, love is kind and is not jealous;
love does not brag and is not arrogant, does not act unbecomingly;
it does not seek its own, is not provoked,
does not take into account a wrong suffered,
does not rejoice in unrighteousness, but rejoices with the truth . . ."
1 Corinthians 13:4-6

During this very painful vehicle experience, I was also beginning to see a lot of stuff rise to the surface in me that I was not at all proud of. I wondered: *How did You do it, Jesus? How did You love those who persecuted You? How did You "do good" to those who spitefully used You?*

Oh! To love as Jesus loved did not feel good to my nature. Yet, somehow, deep down inside of me, I truly sensed that Jeff's plan was indeed God's heart for us in this circumstance. So after regrouping from Jeff's additional news about "sowing seeds," I finally came to terms with all of it.

Whew! This was hard; a huge test of faith for me.

I honestly didn't know if I could trust the Lord completely and wholeheartedly with this, but I would try. What choice did I have? We had committed to the plan, the decision had been made, and we were going forward with it.

Jeff went to the auto repair shop.

With KFC in hand for the owner and employees, Jeff told the man that after much prayer and discussion he and I had decided to give the van to him to keep, along with the cash to get it titled. He explained that we really couldn't afford to have the van repaired, and that perhaps he could repair it for the shop to use as a loaner . . .

When Jeff got home I was full of questions. The biggest one on my mind—and the first one I asked—was, "How did he respond to all that you did for him?" thinking to myself that surely the man's initial response would match mine—shock; then total gratitude would flow from him for our generosity.

Uh-uh.

Jeff simply said the shop owner was "somewhat nonchalant," and that he had basically just said thank you, with no show of emotion whatsoever, and no other thoughts of gratitude.

My thoughts and emotions collided. *Just a small, simple thank you? As if this kind of thing took place on a daily basis? Like it was a normal occurrence for someone to just walk into the shop and hand over their vehicle, for keeps, along with their cash, AND lunch as well?!*

I was a bit frustrated by the man's apparent lack of appreciation.

Jeff tried to appease me by telling me not to worry about it and assured me again that we had done the right thing.

I felt the Holy Spirit convicting me that it was not my place to judge the shop owner or his response—in the same way in which it was not the place of others to judge me, the very issues which had so deeply hurt me through the years. I was simply to walk in obedience to what we believed the Lord had told us to do, and that worrying about what kind of response the man showed—or did not show—should not be the motive of my heart toward giving.

Ouch!

I knew these things were true and that I needed to be reminded of them. I certainly felt like I was in a season of pruning, and while much growth takes place after the pruning is complete, it can certainly be painful in the process! But again, God always has our best interest at heart and sometimes has to reveal to us the condition and motive of our hearts so He can do an even greater work in and through us, for His glory.

So there we were. We had obeyed God by doing what we felt He had prompted in us; now we were in another difficult season: waiting for His provision for a second vehicle. Thankfully the waiting only lasted about a week, but it sure felt like an eternity to me!

Jeff, to his credit, remained pretty peaceful through the week. I can't say the same about myself so much. We were currently down to one car, still borrowing the neighbor's car, and I was beginning to waver in my faith again, wondering how long this would continue.

One evening, I somewhat sarcastically piped up and asked Jeff if he thought God was just going to drop a new car in our driveway, or perhaps someone would just walk up to us and give us a set of keys.

Not long after, I was again convicted. I felt *awful* that I had said those things (in that tone) to my husband, knowing he was doing his best to be obedient to God and patient in waiting to discern from Him what our next step should be. I realized I had been speaking to Jeff out of fear and doubt, second-guessing whether or not we had truly heard from God and had made the right decisions. I had vented my frustrations on the man I loved most!

Taking the plunge to give our van away began to seem like an easier thing than the long, painful waiting; then a much-needed distraction came our way.

My grandma invited us to have dinner with her and I was so relieved to get out of the house and hopefully get my mind on something other than our current situation. Avanti's restaurant was on our way to her house, so she asked us to phone-in everyone's order, pick it up, and she would pay us for everything when we got to her place.

The five of us piled happily into Jeff's small work car and headed out to pick up dinner and go see Grandma.

As we pulled into Avanti's parking lot I saw a beautiful Ford Excursion parked in the adjoining lot, with a big FOR SALE sign on the window. I looked admiringly at it but quickly came to the realistic conclusion that an SUV as nice as that one would be way out of our price league. We didn't even *have* much of a price league to begin with.

I tried not to get depressed.

I glanced over at Jeff, wondering if the SUV had caught his eye as well. To my surprise and delight, he commented on what a beautiful vehicle it was and jotted down the phone number displayed. He said we might call about it on the way home, later that evening. Excitement grabbed hold of me.

Needless to say, I was highly distracted throughout our visit with Grandma. All I could really think about was what might transpire when we called about the Excursion on our way home. I tried not to get my hopes up, but it was really difficult. To me, that vehicle was gorgeous; way better than our former minivan. The SUV was big and bold, and I loved it. On top of that, it was one of my favorite colors—a shiny red.

After what felt like hours, we left Grandma's and headed back toward Avanti's to look at the vehicle. My anticipation grew with each mile. Once there, Jeff called the number and about ten minutes later the owner arrived to meet us.

Immediately upon introducing ourselves, I had a really good feeling, like things were falling into place with no straining or striving to make anything happen. My feelings about the vehicle's owner were confirmed when he said that he and his wife no longer needed such a large vehicle. Their children (all but one) had driver's licenses. He then went on to say that the Excursion had been a great blessing to their family and they wanted it to be a blessing for another family now.

This was beginning to feel too good to be true as he agreed to let us take the Excursion for a test drive while he enjoyed a cup of coffee at a nearby shop. He said he had no qualms about us taking a drive (*in his gorgeous SUV*), and told us to take our time. So we left Jeff's work car in the lot and all five climbed in for the test drive.

We were even more impressed with the vehicle as we drove it. It ran great and the interior was immaculate. Thoughts of driving my girls to school, going grocery shopping, running errands, and taking family trips . . . in such luxury, captivated my thoughts like an amazing dream.

We arrived back at the parking lot and discussed the price with the owner. To our surprise, he was asking a lot less than we had anticipated. We shared our situation with him, and that we loved the vehicle, but we were not sure if we could get the financing or a manageable monthly payment. We asked if he could give us a couple days to discuss it and explore our financial options. He was very nice and understanding and took our name and cell numbers, agreeing to call us first if he got any other calls of serious interest about the SUV. He also told us that he owned his own business and considered himself a pretty good judge of character and said he felt good about us.

Things seemed to be falling into place and I couldn't help but wonder, *Could this be what God has for us?*

Over the course of the next couple of days, Jeff and I discussed the possibility and the financial practicalities of purchasing that vehicle. Our biggest dilemma, of course, was the financing and the monthly payment amount. With our present bills, we didn't have much income left over to budget in a car payment.

Jeff inquired at his place of employment about taking a loan against his retirement. Shortly after, we were told in detail what would be involved and surprisingly discovered that we could do this! The monthly payment for the loan was going to be far less than we had assumed for that vehicle's type and year.

After prayer and continued discussion, we felt comfortable with the financing option and stepped out in faith again. We called the vehicle owner and a few days later we were seated at our bank, completing the purchase paperwork.

I was so excited!

As we were meeting with our loan officer, she pulled up the fair market value for that Excursion's factors. After running the numbers she raised her eyebrows in surprise and said, "You're getting a good deal!" With the towing package and all the extras on that particular vehicle, we learned it was worth about $2,250 more than what we were purchasing it for!

God is good!!

Jeff and I just smiled at each other knowingly. God had done this amazing thing for us. We were so grateful—and humbled.

We got another surprise from God that evening. After doing some quick math, Jeff discovered that $2,250 was almost exactly what we had gifted to the owner of the auto shop—combining the worth of our old van with the cash we'd given him, plus the cost of the chicken dinner for the owner and his employees.

Wow!

We don't believe in coincidences—at all. We knew it was God, our Abba, who had more than blessed us for being obedient to His promptings to give selflessly and generously to others—despite my displeasing roller coaster of emotions and vacillating faith.

He's good even when we're not.

Every time I looked at my shiny red SUV, I was reminded of God's goodness and His "exceedingly abundant" provision in our life—just as He had provided so abundantly for Abraham, and Hannah, of the Old Testament.

I was reminded through our circumstance that at times it may feel as though God is withholding His blessings when we don't see our dreams and desires coming to pass, or as quickly as we would like or hope; but God sees the beginning to the end. He ultimately has our best interests at heart—"in all things."

The Word says He is "able to do exceeding abundantly above all that we ask or think" (Ephesians 3:20 KJV). This does not mean that we will always get what we want, or think we need, for our Abba truly knows what is best for His children. His plans for our lives are much higher and greater than our own human reasoning and thinking, and His blessings far exceed our imaginations. He is Abba and He is good.

Chapter 12

Forgiving and Releasing Those Who have Hurt You

One of my final steps in dealing with the root of rejection was forgiving and releasing those who had hurt me. This proved to require much from me; but in the end it was freeing. It brought the healing, wholeness, and peace in my life I so desperately longed for but had not been able to attain for so many years.

When we live holding grudges and hanging onto unforgiveness toward those who have hurt or offended us, it's only ourselves we are punishing, not our offenders. More often than not the offenders have no idea they have even wronged or hurt us, and they're not suffering in the least bit.

Our prayers can remain hindered when we're harboring unforgiveness. God's Word tells us that He won't forgive our sins until we've first forgiven the sins of others.

"But if you do not forgive men their sins,
your Father will not forgive your sins."
Matthew 6:15 (NIV)

If we're in need of physical healing, this can also be blocked by our unforgiving hearts. Jesus said, "Therefore, confess your sins to one another, and pray for one another so that you may be healed. The effective prayer of a righteous man can accomplish much" (James 5:16).

God's desire is that we all live in unity with each other, not in strife and with unforgiveness. "Behold, how good and how pleasant it is for brothers to dwell together in unity" (Psalm 133:1)! When possible, live at peace with all men."

Likewise, Hebrews 12:14 says, "Pursue peace with all men, and the sanctification without which no one will see the Lord."

Our forgiveness of others will not only help us to better "see the Lord," but will also help others to better see Him while freeing ourselves from the mental and emotional bondage of anguish, anger, and resentment planted in us by the offense.

Forgiving and releasing others in our hearts and minds, frees us to become all God intended us to be. Forgiveness is **not** condoning the offense, but freeing ourselves from the cancerous emotions festering inside us. To free ourselves, anger and resentment is rooted out by the act of forgiving.

You see, forgiveness is not about the offender, it's about our own freedom of heart and mind.

It's not always easy to forgive. At times it's a process. Based on the depth and longevity of the hurt, the act of forgiving may be one we must practice over and over to become completely free.

Striving to forgive someone oftentimes feels contrary to our conscious choice to forgive; but the act of forgiving is also not about how we feel emotionally about the offense or the offender. Forgiveness is about freeing ourselves from the emotional and mental root of turmoil.

We may still feel the sting of the wound, but as we choose to forgive, as an act of our will, the negative root of hurt, anger, and resentment is no longer being fed, by us, and will eventually die.

The act of forgiving and releasing offenders is one way in which we become transformed by renewing our *mind.* And we do this by taking every *thought* captive to the obedience of Christ.

Finally, the act of forgiving is a command. Christ says that we must forgive others for Him to forgive us for our own sins; for we are all sinners.

Forgiving and obeying God is a choice; an act of our will.

What has been helpful in my life toward consciously choosing to forgive is verbally saying out loud to God, "Lord, I forgive (him or her) and their actions against me. I release them and this burden into Your hands." As hard as this was in the beginning, I learned to pray blessings over the very people who had wronged me and prayed that God would help me love them as He does.

"But I say to you, love your enemies
and pray for those who persecute you."
Matthew 5:44

I found my heart softening and changing toward those who had wounded me as I began to intercede for them in prayer, with an attitude of forgiveness in my mind, as a decision I was making. I also asked God to help me see each individual as He does—with love and compassion—and to give me His compassion and heart for them. He's been so faithful to answer this prayer.

Again, forgiving does *not* mean we condone the wrong; but nor does it mean we allow ourselves to become a doormat—allow people to "walk all over us." And it doesn't mean we do not still need to keep healthy boundaries intact. In fact, sometimes when an offense has taken place, the boundaries must be enforced to an even greater degree—as with our neighbors' John and Sally—to help prevent the same offense from happening again; and to further help the offender realize that there will be consequences for unacceptable behavior. But agape love—not anger—should be the driving force behind setting and enforcing healthy boundaries, just as agape love and obedience to God is the driving force behind forgiving. Agape love is selfless, sacrificial, unconditional love; the highest form of love; God's holy love.

"You have heard that it was said, 'An eye for an eye,
and a tooth for a tooth.'
But I say to you, do not resist an evil person;
but whoever slaps you on
your right cheek, turn the other to him also."
Matthew 5:38-39

I've learned that if I've been wounded or treated unjustly, vengeance is God's – not mine. The apostle Paul reminds us of God's command, "Never take your own revenge, beloved, but leave room for the wrath of God, for it is written, 'Vengeance is Mine, I will repay,' says the Lord" (Romans 12:19).

As I shared previously, there have been several situations in my life when those closest to me have criticized, accused, and spoken out against me in judgment. These were such painful experiences and I felt so rejected. With everything in me, I wanted to defend myself against the accusations and hurtful words. But, as I sought the Lord before responding, I often sensed His still, small voice speaking to me: "Angie, if you defend yourself, then I cannot defend you."

"Blessed are you when people insult you and persecute you, and falsely
say all kinds of evil
against you because of Me. Rejoice and be glad, for your reward in
heaven is great;
for in the same way they persecuted the prophets
who were before you."
Matthew 5:12

I knew that God could indeed defend me a lot better than I could defend myself, but would I *allow* Him to do this? I chose to take my hands out of the situations where I was hurt and focus my time and attitude on forgiving (though reluctantly at times), and to *trust* God to make things right where people had wronged me.

In all honesty, there were times I felt as though the situation was going from bad to worse and I would begin to second-guess my decision to let God defend me, simply because He wasn't always "speedy" enough for me. I would get tired of waiting. But He says, "Let us not lose heart in doing good, for in due time we will reap if we do not grow weary" (Galatians 6:9).

Sometimes I wondered if "due time" would ever come. But I know that God's timetable is different from mine. My part is to forgive and to trust in Him.

I saw time and time again how He was faithful to defend me, and each time it strengthened my faith in Him and encouraged my heart with reminders of His promises.

Often, after coming out of difficult circumstances, God would reveal to me much later how He had been working on and softening a person's heart regarding a situation—although, in the middle of the circumstance, there appeared to be no change was taking place.

Trusting in God's divinity in all things is the key, "'For man looks at the outward appearance, but the Lord looks at the heart'" (1 Samuel 16:7).

God often works behind the scenes in our lives. He says, "We see through a glass, darkly . . ." (1 Corinthians 13:12 KJV). Oftentimes, we can't see the bigger picture until much later. It's in the dry times of our lives (when it appears as though He's doing nothing) that we can grow and learn to trust Him to a greater degree.

During the final stage of writing this book, ironically, I experienced several very personal circumstances of hurt and rejection which I had to forgive and release to God. As I questioned the Lord, bringing to Him my feelings of betrayal, rejection, and confusion, I'd pray: "Lord, I've gone to the person and I've done what I clearly heard you tell me, so why are they responding this way?"

I could sense His heart telling me that He, too, knew what it was like to be rejected. Hebrews 5:8 says, "Although He was a Son, He learned obedience from the things which He suffered." Isaiah 53:3 also shows how Jesus was rejected by men: "He was despised and forsaken of men, a man of sorrows and acquainted with grief; and like one from whom men hide their face He was despised, and we did not esteem Him."

Although He could relate to the very things I was suffering, He still expected me to be obedient to Him by forgiving.

I learned that no matter how people may respond to me or even reject me, He, the Lord, my Abba, will never reject me. His promise is that He will never leave me or forsake me.

I've come to realize that I'm simply responsible for *obeying* what God has placed on my heart – not for another person's reactions or responses. Those are their own choices.

It would sometimes seem that the more others disapproved of me, or the choices I was making for my life, the more favor and approval I'd sense from the Lord when responding to the individuals as He would have me respond: with agape love and forgiveness. I learned that I couldn't seek both God's approval and man's approval at the same time; therefore I had to release all people to Him.

For years, fear of man held me in such bondage. I was consumed with the thoughts and opinions people might have of me, and I was constantly striving to please *everybody* so I wouldn't feel the sting of their rejection. But over time—through this long journey of dealing with the root of rejection in me—I came to the place of wanting nothing more than to please God and to become whole and healed in every way. I was no longer allowing my thoughts to be negatively controlled and consumed when people hurt or rejected me.

Forgiving and releasing others, and forgiving myself, was part of me becoming free in heart and mind. I had to learn to let go of the things in my past that I was ashamed of and embed God's truth inside me: **the old me had been made new** by Christ's love and forgiveness for me. As a new creation in Christ, I could no longer define myself by my circumstances, but rather by my identity in Christ, rooted and grounded in Him alone.

"Therefore if anyone is in Christ, he is a new creature; the old things passed away; behold, new things have come."
2 Corinthians 5:17

There was a time in my life when I was bitter and resentful against the rejection and hard trials I had experienced, but now I can actually thank God that, through those circumstances, He gave me the grace and strength to endure and grow. It was those very circumstances of hardship that He used to build character and perseverance in me, and an unwavering faith in Him, which gave me the strength to forgive and release those in my life who had hurt me in any way—great or small. I am a stronger person for those experiences and can now see how Christ works in all things for my good.

When I think back to my adolescent years—the betrayal of those I had considered my 'friends,' and the slippery path of destruction I was on—I remembered contemplating taking my life. I believed the lie that there was no hope for me and things would never get better. Now, I see more clearly the transforming journey He had me on and how He had walked beside me all along, never leaving me, never forsaking me, and never once rejecting me. He had truly been the friend that has stuck closer than a brother.

"A man of too many friends comes to ruin,
But there is a friend who sticks closer than a brother."
Proverbs 18:24

In and through Him, He has not only allowed me to deal with the root of rejection and learn how to forgive people, but also, by His grace, He's allowed me to help others see that they, too, can experience freedom from rejection and the freedom which comes from forgiving and releasing others.

"I waited patiently for the Lord; and He inclined to
me and heard my cry.
He brought me up out of the pit of destruction,
out of the miry clay,
and He set my feet upon a rock
making my footsteps firm. He put a
new song in my mouth, a song of praise to our God;
many will see and fear and will trust in the Lord."
Psalm 40:1-3

Chapter 13

The Confident Woman

For most of my life I had put my confidence in things that are temporal, ever fading away—such as my physical appearance, material possessions, how I performed . . . But as God continued His work in me, I began to see that true value and worth, which produces a steadfast and Godly confidence, are not found in earthly things or in others, but in Christ alone.

Much of my earlier life was an example of how the evil one is always "seeking whom he may devour," working to rob us of our destinies in Christ. (1 Peter 5:8)

As I grew in Christ, I learned that my confidence increased when I "fought the good fight of faith" for my destiny, by being yoked together with Christ. (1 Timothy 6:12)

Fulfilling God's destiny for our lives is not something that is simply handed over to us. It takes determination, perseverance, work, and the "fight of faith" to hold on to it and see it to completion. That's why the Word says, "continue to work out your salvation" (Philippians 2:12 NIV). This isn't referring to the new birth we gain in Christ when we've accepted Him as Savior, but to the continuing spiritual growth we gain as believers while working to fulfill the purposes for which God created us.

I had to ask myself, *How badly do I want confidence in Christ? How much of myself am I willing to invest?*

That which costs us nothing is usually
not appreciated or of much value;
but that which costs us everything matters greatly.
These are the things we're usually
willing to fight for.

Matthew 13:46 examples this truth: "Upon finding one pearl of great value, he went and sold all that he had and bought it."

Toward the final stages of writing this book, the temptation was there to quit. Writing was grueling. It was hard. It seemed like I had so far yet to go to reach the finish line, but the Lord began to encourage me to put my trust and confidence in *Him alone*—not in myself or others.

"For we are the true circumcision,
who worship in the Spirit of God
and glory in Christ Jesus and put no confidence in the flesh."
Philippians 3:3

It was not even my idea to write this book; it was the Lord's plan, one of His purposes for my life. And I had to remind myself (more often than not) that He would be faithful to complete the good work He had begun in me.

"For I am confident of this very thing,
that He who began a good work in you
will perfect it until the day of Christ Jesus."
Philippians 1:6

In order to gain this confidence, I learned that I must *partner with Him* and be faithful to do my part. Just as parents have for our children, God has expectations and requirements for us, as our Abba, that's presented to us throughout His Word. To write this book to completion meant writing even when I was weary. It meant pushing past my insecurities and the skills I felt I lacked. It meant asking others for help where and when I needed it and persevering even in the smallest things.

It meant giving myself wholeheartedly to the Lord in faith, with reckless abandonment to "self." It meant believing and having the full confidence that He would be faithful to supply all that I needed to carry out this task.

God is faithful! He equips us and supplies us with all that we need to succeed to finish the race He's set before us; completing all that He has called us to complete. Our part is being willing to push past the distractions and willing to sacrifice our time and resources to give ourselves totally to what He has purposed in us—regardless of how great or small it may seem to us.

Our part is not looking back, but putting our hands to the plow with our full confidence in the Lord, diligent with what He's placed before us.

To gain the confidence God intended for me to have in Him, I had come face-to-face with the root of rejection I had carried for much of my life. I had to take an honest look at the things in my life that were giving me a temporary and false sense of confidence, and I had to put all those things in their rightful place: below my relationship with God, below my relationship with my husband, below my relationship with my children and others. And I had to allow the Lord to begin to fill all the holes and empty places in my heart that had grown deeper in me through the years.

Becoming a confident woman of God required that I meditate on His truths and keep them deep inside me—especially on the days when I felt unlovely. The truth of how Christ sees me as His child, His daughter, is exampled in Song of Solomon: "You are altogether beautiful, my darling, and there is no blemish in you" (Song of Solomon 4:7).

As wonderful as my husband Jeff is, and as much as I deeply appreciate the countless times he sincerely compliments me and tells me I'm beautiful, I learned that true confidence comes in knowing and believing the truths of God's Word about me: I am His beloved daughter and beautiful in His sight because I have been washed clean by the blood of Christ. I am forgiven and He makes me free because I have placed my hope and trust in HIM.

Becoming a confident woman of God meant that I had to understand in the core of my being that true beauty, wholeness, peace, freedom, and confidence come from the inside out by being rooted in Christ—the everlasting Vine.

"I am the vine; you are the branches.
If a man remains in me and I in him, he will bear much fruit;
apart from me you can do nothing."
John 15:5

As I began to see myself and others through the eyes of God, I saw true and lasting beauty. As I spent time in getting to know others for who God created them to be, I saw past their outward, physical appearances, to their heart—the real person inside who transcends physical appearances. Proverbs 27:19 (NIV) says, "As water reflects the face, So one's life reflects the heart."

God had patiently revealed to me over time that no matter what my bathroom scale showed, and no matter how I perceived myself when I looked into the mirror . . . , I would become a confident woman when I truly saw myself as He sees me: forgiven, free, whole, and beautiful from the inside out.

Even the most seemingly insignificant issues were transformed to real freedom in me. For example, I was able to go out to pick up my girls from school or run to the grocery store without putting on makeup, perfecting my hair . . . While I still desired and enjoyed looking nice on the outside, my outward appearance was no longer a driving force toward confidence. I had to learn that my true beauty, worth, and confidence comes from Christ living in me and me being rooted in Him, the Vine.

I grew to understand that I didn't have to strive to earn God's love or acceptance. His love is a free gift and He never rejects those who have put their faith and trust in His Son, Jesus Christ. Those who are in Christ are eternally sealed* by God, our names are written on the palm of His hand* and in His book of LIFE.* (*Ephesians 1:13; Isaiah 49:16; Revelation 3:5)

As I began to partner with Christ to dig out the root of rejection and hold fast to God's truths, an inner, lasting confidence began to grow in me. I no longer felt like I needed to perform to win the love and acceptance of others, because who I am in Christ is enough.

As all the wonderful truths of God's Word (sprinkled liberally throughout my story) began to take root in me, I began to be transformed into the confident woman God desired me to be. It was truly liberating.

I learned through the journey that when we are truly confident and comfortable with ourselves, knowing who we are in Christ, others are more comfortable around us. I realized a lot of the pressure I had been putting on myself through the years was due to me taking myself, my humanness and fallibility, too seriously in the insignificant things of life. If I made a mistake, forgot something, or said something foolish, it actually began to feel okay in me to laugh at myself! What a transformation! Laughter releases a great deal of unnecessary pressure that we place on ourselves when we're striving for human perfection. Laughter is one of God's gifts to us. It's good and healthy for us to laugh.

"A joyful heart makes a cheerful face . . ."
Proverbs 15:13

Another aspect of becoming a confident woman was the ability to rejoice and celebrate in the successes and victories of those closest to me, without feeling threatened by their achievements—thinking I was not as talented or smart in comparison. I had learned that God does not compare me with others. We're each a unique creation by His design.

When we're living with the root of rejection, it's easy for us to feel threatened or wounded when those near us succeed. But when we're rooted in the Vine—drawing true, nurturing life and confidence from the fullness of Christ—we can sincerely rejoice in and celebrate the victories of others and truly be happy for them.

I no longer felt threatened when those in my life excelled me. I was able to truly rejoice with them, seeing God's purposes being fulfilled in their lives.

When we are truly confident—being rooted in the Vine—we will cheer for others as they go into their God-given destinies. We'll do what we can to partner with them and help propel them forward. We'll not try to hold them back. An example of this is our three girls. Jeff and I determined as parents to speak into our daughters' lives on a daily basis; to encourage them that they could ". . . do all things through Him [Christ] who strengthens . . ." (Philippians 4:13). We challenged them to go for their dreams and taught them who they are in Christ. We let them know that God had a distinctive purpose for their lives and that we believed in them. We told them often that we believed in them. Our desire was for our girls to each become a confident woman of God.

When my oldest daughter, Courtney, graduated eighth grade, I was humbled and amazed to see the work of God unfold in her life so vibrantly. She had been one of two honor students in her eighth grade class.

On graduation night she received four additional awards, including Student of the Year, and she gave a speech to a full auditorium! I was in awe of how she used the platform with such Godly grace, confidence and humility to glorify God and publicly honor her dad and me. She thanked us for believing in her and standing by her side—even through the hard times. She shared how much our words of encouragement meant to her.

She encouraged a full auditorium of people to go for their dreams and spoke into their lives by saying that each person there had a purpose and a destiny.

Wow! What a ripple effect our lives and actions can have on others.

I saw this truth first hand as I listened to Courtney speak the very words Jeff and I had spoken into her through the years. I realized that the tide was indeed turning for the next generation as she entered high school. She was excelling and going in a completely different direction than I had at her age. I was amazed and so thankful that my mistakes and the sins of my youth were not being repeated in the next generation, but rather that God's blessings were on our daughters and they were already realizing the confidence they have in Christ.

I was finally experiencing God's restoration, not only through what He had done in me but also through my children's successes. I celebrated their victories with them, and let them know how very proud I was of them.

God is so good. He's so faithful. He can bring restoration and true confidence into our lives that we never thought possible.

The confident woman is not one who places her identity in the thoughts and opinions of others, nor in physical appearance, earthly achievements, or fame. The confident woman is not one who measures herself by her status or wealth, or who seeks earthly treasures.

The confident woman is not one of self-pride but humble righteousness in Christ.

The confident woman is one who has placed her full trust in God through Jesus Christ and one who serves Him and others—our true purpose.

The confident woman is one who is rooted in the Vine and who lives in the purposes and plans of God for her life, allowing Him to be rooted in her to carry out His divine destiny as God generously elaborates in Proverbs 31:10-31.

The confident woman is one who truly knows who she in Christ, and who He is in her: the Vine.

His love and faithfulness is truly *everlasting*!

CPSIA information can be obtained at www.ICGtesting.com
Printed in the USA
LVOW08s1329290816

502319LV00002B/75/P